what you say is what you get!

Don Gossett

SPIRE BOOKS

Fleming H. Revell Company ● Old Tappan, New Jersey

Other books by the author:

PRAISE AVENUE
THERE'S DYNAMITE IN PRAISE

WHAT YOU SAY IS WHAT YOU GET

Don Gossett's addresses:

Box 2
Blaine, Washington 98230

Box 1177, Cloverdale
Surrey, British Columbia
CANADA V3S 4R1

Copyright © 1976 by Don Gossett
Printed in the United States of America
ISBN: 8007-8382-4

Unless otherwise indicated, all Scripture quotations in this volume are from the King James Version of the Bible.

CONTENTS

PART I. WHAT YOU SAY

PART II. WHAT YOU GET

PART I

WHAT YOU SAY

Chapter One

HOW I DISCOVERED THE POWER OF WHAT YOU SAY

The year I discovered the importance of what some people call "mere" words was the hardest year in my entire life: the whole year was filled with heartache and trouble.

August came and on the fifteenth our daughter, Jeanne Michelle, was born. It was a very difficult delivery for my wife. Our regular doctor was away. His replacement, a confirmed alcoholic, came to see my wife when she first entered the hospital, but his compulsion to drink caused him to be away when the actual time for the delivery arrived.

My wife was kept in the delivery room for a long time, while the nurses tried frantically to locate a doctor. I realized there was some sort of crisis going on, so I prayed earnestly.

Finally, they found a doctor, and Jeanne was delivered. However, it was immediately apparent that she was neither as well nor as strong as our other babies had been.

The doctor told us that my wife had apparently developed a severe calcium deficiency while carrying the baby. Calcium had then gone from baby to mother, causing the bones in the baby's hands and feet to be soft and malformed. He told us the hands could probably be massaged gradually back into place, but that clubbed feet—the kind Jeanne was born with—were generally irreversible even with surgery. On top of that, the baby had developed respiration difficulties, and he could not promise that she would live. She was in critical condition.

Casts were placed on Jeanne's feet, she was placed in an incubator for her respiration, and a special nurse was assigned to massage her hands daily. We had to leave her behind in the hospital when I took my wife home.

Because my wife was still quite weak from giving birth, I was the one who went to the hospital every day to visit the baby. I would sit beside the incubator and watch her kick her tiny feet, knocking the plaster casts together. I was only allowed to hold her for a few precious moments each day, so I spent most of the time praying, asking God to touch this little one and give her health and strength.

Finally, we were able to bring Jeanne home. It would almost break my heart to hear her casts bang together when she would kick her tiny feet. It seemed as though God was permitting Satan to test our faith and dedication to the limit.

During this time, my wife was stricken with rheumatic fever. Our doctor told us that her illness had been caused by the same calcium deficiency which had caused the baby's clubbed feet.

I had to leave the field of evangelism and devote my time to caring for my wife and our three children. Besides Jeanne, there were also our two-year-old son, Michael, and our one-year-old daughter, Judy. Since I had three babies to care for, I would often prepare bottles for all three of them at the same time. In spite of Jeanne's condition, I often thought what a beautiful sight it was to see all three of the babies that God had given us!

During this time, our troubles caused my wife and me to grow closer to the Lord than ever before. We studied the Bible extensively and read many good faith-building books, pamphlets, and magazines.

Some weeks after we brought her home, Jeanne's feet had grown so quickly that it was time to remove the casts and replace them with larger ones. When Dr. Graham, our regular doctor, removed the casts, *Jeanne's feet were perfectly straight.*

Doctor Graham told us that he had never known of a case in which clubbed feet became completely straight. In fact, he said, "She was not well when she was born, and there wasn't a lot of hope for her survival. Now she is completely well. Both her feet are perfectly normal. Her respiration is fine. All I can say is that I'm glad it happened."

Although we knew that we had seen a miracle, we were saddened by the fact that my wife continued to suffer with rheumatic fever. She grew much worse, and suffered from excruciating pain day and night. It seemed likely that our miracle baby would lose her mother.

Weeks passed, and I had no income at all. I mortgaged our furniture, but the money went very quickly. Because of her condition, I couldn't leave my wife alone, and I had no money to hire someone to stay with her. Again and again I asked God to see us through.

One unforgettable evening I was reading Psalm 27 to my wife, when suddenly the Holy Spirit quickened this scripture to me. I turned excitedly to her and said, "Honey, did you hear that?"

"Hear what, Don?"

She had allowed her mind to wander as I had been reading. I couldn't blame her. She had lain bedfast for months with rheumatic fever. Her skin was discolored, her feet and legs were swollen twice their size, and her strength was slowly and surely ebbing. Despite the fact that many of our friends had come to visit and to pray for her, there had been no permanent improvement. The outlook was so dark that we feared the Angel of Death was at our door. We were undergoing a real trial of faith.

That night, as she looked up questioningly, I leaped from my chair, repeating the first verse of Psalm 27: "The Lord is the strength of my life!" As these words came alive to me, I hugged my wife as I said it again, "Honey, did you *hear* that scripture? The Lord is the strength of *your* life!"

Quietly she repeated these words aloud: "The Lord is the strength of my life." As the Spirit brought these words to life for her, the listless look faded from her eyes, and with a vibrancy that I had not heard for a long, long time, she exclaimed, "Yes, I *do* see it! The Lord *is* the strength of my life!"

A joy such as I had not felt for months surged

through me. I could hardly stand still as I shouted, "Honey, if the Lord is the strength of your life, then you don't have to lie there in that bed! You don't have to stay weak and sick! In Jesus' name you can get up and walk!"

"Get up and walk, after all these months in bed?" Her face looked puzzled. Then, trustingly, she slowly drew herself up. I began to see an expression of belief replace the doubt and distress on her face. As she struggled to her feet, she cried out exultantly, "The Lord is the strength of my life!"

I could clearly see that she was aching as much as ever, and that her feet were still swollen as she put them on the floor. But now she had forgotten herself. She was not going by how she felt. She was thinking of, relying on, the mighty, infallible Word of God. And now she was calling out boldly, "The Lord is the strength of my life," claiming God's strength to heal her own weak body.

She stepped out from her bed. As she began to walk across the room without wavering, she continued joyously to repeat, "The Lord is the strength of my life! The Lord is the strength of my life!"

The more she repeated God's Word, the more my wife received God's strength. Right before our eyes, the pain left, the swelling receded, and the discoloration faded. Two medical doctors would verify that she has been completely healed of crippling, killing rheumatic fever. Never from that joyous day until this has she ever again suffered from that horrible disease.

The night my wife was healed of rheumatic fever was the night that I began to realize that *What You Say Is What You Get*.

I believe we get what we say because God honors His Word—and His Word says that "whosoever . . . shall believe that those things which he saith shall come to pass . . . shall have whatsoever he saith" (Mark 11:23).

He shall have whatsoever he saith! That is an awesome Bible promise. How awesome, it took me some time to realize. Solomon said, "Whoso keepeth his mouth and his tongue, keepeth his soul from troubles" (Proverbs 21:23). And Jesus said, "That every idle word that men shall speak, they shall give account thereof in the day of judgment. For by thy words thou shalt be justified, and by thy words thou shalt be condemned" (Matthew 12:36, 37).

In spite of the fact, however, that I was familiar with these well-known biblical quotations, it had somehow never occurred to me that the promise, "he shall have whatsoever he saith," was a two-edged sword: it could work for me, or it could work against me, *depending on what I said*.

One day back in 1961 the Lord spoke to me, just as He spoke to His people long ago. He quoted Scripture to me. First He said, "Ye have wearied the Lord with your words" (Malachi 2:17). Then He spoke to me again, saying, "Your words have been stout against Me, saith the Lord" (Malachi 3:13). I was shocked! How had I wearied the Lord? I couldn't imagine how my words could have been stout against Him—surely I could never have said anything against my Lord!

As I pondered about what the Lord could possibly mean, the Holy Spirit, our Great Teacher, brought to my attention that I had developed a negative pattern of speech. I constantly used phrases like "I can't" and "I'm afraid," when God's Word told me "I can" and "Fear not." My words were out of harmony with God's Word; I was disagreeing with the Lord!

"Can two walk together except they be agreed?" asks Amos 3:3. I discovered that I could never walk with God in blessing, triumph, and abundant supply as long as I disagreed with God's Word. So here was the secret: I had to agree with the Lord. I had to say what God said about my life. I needed to say what He said about my health, my finances, my strength, my anointing, my power, about all of the blessings He had promised me in His Word.

As the Holy Spirit was reproving me, He also led me to write in my diary, for my own admonition, my "Never Again List." I have reproduced this list at the end of this chapter. At that time, I would never have dreamed that later, the Holy Spirit would lead me to publish this "Never Again List" in many languages, sharing it with hundreds and thousands of people all over the world.

Praise God, it is true that if you believe what you are saying, *What You Say Is What You Get*. If you say, "I can't pay my bills," for instance, you won't be able to pay your bills—even though God's Word says that "My God shall supply all your need according to his riches in glory by Christ Jesus" (Philippians 4:19). But if you change your negative way of speaking (and thinking), based on God's promise to supply, you will receive the financial miracle you need.

This whole book is entirely on how to get what you say. But before I explain how to get what you say, I wanted to get in one word of warning: *since what you say is what you get, don't ever say anything you wouldn't want to get.* To help you overcome any habit of negative speaking, it may help you to start where I started: with my "Never Again List."

MY NEVER AGAIN LIST

Never Again will I confess "I can't," for "I can do all things through Christ which strengtheneth me" (Philippians 4:13).

Never Again will I confess lack, for "My God shall supply all of my need according to His riches in glory by Christ Jesus" (Philippians 4:19).

Never Again will I confess fear, for "God hath not given me the spirit of fear, but of power, and of love, and of a sound mind" (2 Timothy 1:7).

Never Again will I confess doubt and lack of faith, for "God hath given to every man the measure of faith" (Romans 12:3).

Never Again will I confess weakness, for "The Lord is the strength of my life" (Psalm 27:1) and "The people that know their God shall be strong and do exploits" (Daniel 11:32).

Never Again will I confess supremacy of Satan over my life, for "Greater is he that is within me than he that is in the world" (1 John 4:4).

Never Again will I confess defeat, for "God always causeth me to triumph in Christ Jesus" (2 Corinthians 2:14).

Never Again will I confess lack of wisdom, for "Christ Jesus is made unto me wisdom from God" (1 Corinthians 1:30).

Never Again will I confess sickness, for "With His stripes I am healed" (Isaiah 53:5), and Jesus "Himself took my infirmities and bare my sicknesses" (Matthew 8:17).

Never Again will I confess worries and frustrations, for I am "Casting all my cares upon him who careth for me" (1 Peter 5:7). In Christ I am "care-free!"

Never Again will I confess bondage, for "Where the Spirit of the Lord is, there is liberty" (2 Corinthians 3:17). My body is the temple of the Holy Spirit!

Never Again will I confess condemnation, for "There is therefore now no condemnation to them which are in Christ Jesus" (Romans 8:1). I am in Christ; therefore, I am free from condemnation.

Chapter Two

YOUR INVISIBLE MEANS
OF SUPPORT

Mabel Marvin, who attended one of my services, shared with me a good example of the results that can come from taking God at His Word. She and her husband triumphed over a very bad situation just by refusing to give way to negative thoughts and words and by declaring out loud their positive faith in God's provision.

I have a pretty good idea that Satan was more than ordinarily busy the day this story started because it was a Sunday, at a time when people were on their way home from church. He must have been aware that he would have to work harder than on other days to counteract what God's people had been hearing in church. He was probably watching Mabel's situation gleefully, but he didn't reckon with Mabel, who knew the power of the spoken word, when used according to God's principles. Here is Mabel's story about that situation:

"The sermon that January morning had been about speaking out in positive words when there is trouble—when everything goes wrong. Our minister had told us that since 'we know that all things work together for good to them that love God' (Romans 8:28), we know that God will cause our worst circumstances to work on our behalf, no matter how impossible things may seem at the time. I was about to have an object lesson on the morning's sermon.

"On our way home from church, everything seemed to go wrong. Our old truck, our only means of transportation and the means by which we earned our living delivering milk, broke down again. And the gears had been fixed less than a month before. We were desperate, for those were war days, days of rationing.

"'It's beyond fixing this time,' my husband Henry said. 'I don't know what we'll do now. So many are ahead of me on the priority list that the car dealer told me that it might be two years before I can get a truck. But we need a truck *now*. How will we get to church? How will we get feed for our cows? How will we deliver our milk or get our groceries? I'm sick about this.'

"'With God, all things are possible,' I reminded him. 'We've prayed a long time. Now it's time to praise the Lord for a new truck. Let's put this morning's sermon into practice!'

"Henry looked at me as if I had certainly gone out of my head. He hesitated and then said, 'Suppose that we do, and we *still* don't get a new truck?'

"'How are we ever going to know if we don't try?' I answered. 'I'm going to start praising the Lord right

18

now for a new truck, and I'm not stopping until we get one. The Lord knows our need. He will meet it. God has promised to supply all our need 'according to his riches in glory' (Philippians 4:19).

"It was two miles over two hills—and it was bitter cold. But every step of the way we praised the Lord for a brand-new truck. And the next day I continued to praise the Lord.

"I was on my knees, still praising the Lord when Henry called to tell me he had a new Dodge truck! Mr. Johnson, the man with whom he had ridden to town after our truck had broken down, had stopped at the Dodge agency on an errand. A truck had arrived the afternoon before, but the man who had ordered it had refused it because the wheelbase was too short for him. Mr. Johnson mentioned our need to the dealer, and Henry had a new Dodge truck!"

There are no coincidences with God. Or perhaps I should rephrase that and quote Sam Feldman, a precious Jewish brother in the Lord, who always says that "coincidence is the handiwork of God." Those of us who walk with God have just seen too many "coincidences" after we pray, too many "accidental" answers to prayer, too often, to believe in coincidences. Mabel Marvin had simply learned the power of using words as an instrument of faith to open the door to God's abundant blessings. She had learned that God was her "invisible means of support." How can you learn to make God *your* "invisible means of support?" It's simple—just follow instructions.

If you want to know how to build a fireplace, you get a construction book that tells you how to do it. If you want to learn to make a pie, you go to a cookbook. If you want to know how to have God meet your needs, you go to His instruction manual.

According to the *Reader's Digest*, the great inventor Buckminster Fuller once stated that the trouble with Spaceship Earth is that it didn't come with a book of instructions. He was wrong. Spaceship Earth *does* come with a book of instructions, and that book is the Bible. As far as you and I are concerned, it is a Manufacturer's Handbook that not only tells us how to operate Spaceship Earth and its inhabitants, but it also tells us how to communicate our service requests to our Manufacturer.

First of all, our Handbook tells us, if we're going to ask favors of God, we have to get on speaking terms with Him. Because God won't answer their prayers, many people believe that there is no God. That's like saying Don Gossett doesn't exist, because he didn't answer his telephone! According to our Handbook, however, there is a *reason* why God isn't talking to many people. "Your iniquities have separated between you and your God, and your sins have hid his face from you, that he will not hear" (Isaiah 59:2). God isn't dead—He's just not listening!

How can we get God to listen to us? The Handbook covers that too. First of all, we shouldn't be surprised if God *isn't* listening to us, since the Handbook tells us that "All have sinned" (Romans 3:23). Therefore, if we're having trouble getting through to God, we must ask Him to forgive us, to erase our sins. He can forgive our sins because His Son, Jesus Christ, "took the rap" for us: "The LORD hath laid on him the iniquity of us all" (Isaiah 53:6).

Jesus Christ "took the rap" for the whole world, but in order to take advantage of it, the Bible tells us, we have to take certain steps: "Repent ye therefore, and be converted, that your sins may be blotted out" (Acts 3:19). "Repenting" is deciding to live God's way, asking His forgiveness for any sins we have committed, and—if we have never done so before—asking Jesus Christ to come into our heart and life (Revelation 3:20).

If we have followed these simple steps, "the blood of Jesus Christ his Son cleanseth us from all sin" (1 John 1:7); the Spirit of Christ comes to dwell in us (Romans 8:9); we become God's children and heirs (John 1:12; Romans 8:16, 17); and "Then shalt thou call, and the LORD shall answer; thou shalt cry, and he shall say, Here I am" (Isaiah 58:9).

The man on the street, if he thinks about God at all, probably thinks of Him as his Father. But does God think of *him* as His son? Only if he has come under the Lordship of Jesus Christ by repenting and accepting Jesus as his Lord and Savior. Anyone who has accepted Jesus is one of God's children.

To people who don't know God, or who are newly acquainted with Him, it often comes as a surprise that God invented "red tape." However, God's red tape never gets snarled! The moment you accept Jesus, your name is officially recorded in heaven as one of God's adopted children, in a central registry referred to as the "Lamb's Book of Life." You now have the legal right, so far as God is concerned, to call yourself God's child and heir. And you have the right to claim as your own all the rights and privileges enjoyed by His Son, Jesus Christ. You are a co-heir with Jesus Christ, and may share in all His privileges! No wonder *What You Say Is What You Get!*

When God adopts you, you have a whole new life ahead of you—an eternal one—which is conducted according to rules which are completely different from the rules you followed up till then. Before, you did everything according to the laws of nature. Now—although you can still function according to natural laws—you have a second set of laws at your disposal. As one of God's children, you have the right to function according to His supernatural laws.

Ken Copeland, in one of his books, gave a very good example of how God's supernatural laws may sometimes seem to "break" His natural laws. Ken is a pilot, and knows a lot about airplanes. He pointed out that airplanes seem to "break" the law of gravity. Actually, however, airplanes function according to the law of lift, another natural law which simply transcends the problems presented by the law of gravity. In the same way, God's supernatural laws transcend God's natural laws. In a way known only to God, God's children need only speak and believe, and the thing which they have spoken will come to pass. Praise God, we don't need to know how it works! You don't need to know how lift transcends gravity in order to ride in an airplane, and you don't need to know how the things you say and believe are going to happen. It is enough that they happen!

Just as the world's natural children need to learn how to walk without being toppled by the law of gravity, God's supernatural children also need to learn how to operate His supernatural laws without being toppled by His natural laws. Learning to walk in the Spirit takes time, just as it took time to learn to walk in the flesh. But it is well worth the effort.

PLEASING GOD

1. "I do always those things that please Him" (John 8:29). This is the motivating force of my Christian life: to be a Father-pleaser. To do always those things that please Him!

2. "And whatsoever we ask, we receive of Him, because we keep His commandments, and do those things pleasing in His sight" (1 John 3:22). Answers to prayer are conditioned on doing those things pleasing in His sight. If my prayers are not being answered, I must seek to please Him more, knowing that His eyes are always upon me!

3. "He had this testimony, that he pleased God" (Hebrews 11:5). This is my heart's desire, my bold ambition, that I might have this same testimony: that I please God with my life, my time, my talents, my money, my all!

4. "But without faith it is impossible to please Him" (Hebrews 11:6). Since I can please God only by faith, I shall boldly live the faith life. How? "I live by the faith of the Son of God" (Galatians 2:20). "The Word is nigh me, even in my mouth and in my heart; that is, the Word of faith" (Romans 10:8). "Faith cometh by hearing, and

hearing by the Word of God" (Romans 10:17).

5. "Do I seek to please men? for if I yet pleased men, I should not be the servant of Christ" (Galatians 1:10). As a true believer, above all else, I seek to please my Lord. "Not with eyeservice, as menpleasers" (Ephesians 6:6).

6. "We then that are strong ought to bear the infirmities of the weak, and not to please ourselves. Let everyone of us please his neighbor for his good to edification. For even Christ pleased not Himself" (Romans 15:1-3). Pleasing God means a denial of pleasing myself, in order to minister in Christ's stead to others.

7. "For thus saith the Lord...choose the things that please me" (Isaiah 56:4). I shall choose to do the things that please my Lord. "Whether therefore ye eat, or drink, or whatsoever ye do, do all to the glory of God" (1 Corinthians 10:31). "And whatsoever ye do in word or deed, do all in the name of the Lord Jesus, giving thanks to God and the Father by him (Colossians 3:17). "And whatsoever ye do, do it heartily, as to the Lord, and not unto men, knowing that of the Lord ye shall receive the reward of the inheritance: for ye serve the Lord Christ" (Colossians 3:23-24).

Chapter Three

WHAT TO SAY TO A MOUNTAIN

Countless people limit their happiness and success in life because they never realize the importance of words, words of all kinds. In the eleventh chapter of Mark, there is an interesting story about the power of the spoken word. Jesus and His disciples were on the way from Bethany to Jerusalem, and Jesus was hungry.

> And seeing a fig tree afar off having leaves, he came, if haply he might find any thing thereon: and when he came to it, he found nothing but leaves; for the time of figs was not yet. And Jesus answered and said unto it, No man eat fruit of thee hereafter for ever. And his disciples heard it....

Here was Jesus, talking to a tree! And we know he was talking out loud, too, because "his disciples heard it." Evidently nothing appeared to happen at the very moment he spoke, however, the Bible goes on to tell us what happened the next morning, as

Jesus and his disciples passed by the fig tree again: And in the morning, as they passed by, they saw the fig tree dried up from the roots. And Peter calling to remembrance saith unto him [Jesus], Master, behold, the fig tree which thou cursedst is withered away. And Jesus answering saith unto them, Have faith in God. For verily I say unto you, That *whosoever shall say* unto this mountain, Be thou removed, and be thou cast into the sea; and shall not doubt in his heart, but shall believe that *those things which he saith* shall come to pass, he shall have *whatsoever he saith.* [italics added].

Please notice that in this passage, Jesus talked more about saying than he did about believing!

Kenneth Hagin says that Mark 11:23 is the secret to success in obtaining miracles from God. Another friend of mine, Austin Barton, has a moving testimony of the practicality and power of this particular passage of Scripture. He had suffered several severe heart attacks, followed by a stroke. There seemed to be no hope for his life. Claiming this passage, he simply told his "mountain of damaged heart and impaired health" to be removed, and he became well, to the glory of God. He resumed his ministry, and specialists agree that there is no evidence whatsoever left in his body of the massive heart attacks he has experienced.

This passage from Mark 11 has also been a great source of power in my own life, and I challenge you to remember that "*whosoever shall say . . .* and shall not doubt in his heart, but shall believe that those things which he saith shall come to pass, *he shall have whatsoever he saith."*

Some people have tried to interpret this passage as a reference to praying. Certainly praying has its important place and is a source of tremendous power, but here Jesus is talking about *saying*, not *praying*. Before you can *say* according to this passage, however, there's one more thing you need to know. You need to know how not to doubt in your heart.

Doubt is the opposite of *faith*. How do you have faith? You decide to take God at His Word. How do you doubt? You decide *not* to take God at his Word, or else you fail to make the decision to take God's Word for the matter in question. The decision to have faith—to take God's Word for a matter—must be a firm one. Each time you decide God's Word can't be trusted, you are falling into doubt. That is why James tells us to "ask in faith, nothing wavering. For he that wavereth is like a wave of the sea driven with the wind and tossed. For let not that man think that he shall receive any thing of the Lord. A double minded man is unstable in all his ways" (James 1:6-8).

Having mentioned that we must not waver if we hope to receive something from God, we also need to point out that it is our *faith* that must not waver. Our decision to believe God must remain firm, no matter how frightened or unsure we may *feel* about the outcome of the matter.

The night my wife was healed of rheumatic fever, she felt awful—weak and in pain. She didn't *feel* like the Lord was the strength of her life, but she *believed*

28

it. How did she know He was her strength? He said so in His Word. Since God said so, it had to be true—no matter what evidence her body offered to the contrary.

The Bible says that God "calleth those things which be not as though they were," (Romans 4:17). God doesn't lie—He just does things differently from the way we do them. Our way is to see and then believe—like doubting Thomas. God's way is to believe and then to see. God says, "Blessed are they that have not seen, and yet have believed" (John 21:29).

In Mark 11:23, there are only two conditions given to receiving "whatsoever" you say. One is believing: you have to believe in your heart that what you say will come to pass. The other is speaking: you have to say the thing you are believing in order for the thing which you say to happen.

Many people think that they need "great faith" in order to have their words work miracles. This is not what Jesus taught, however. He said, "If ye have faith as a grain of mustard seed [a very small seed] ye shall say unto this mountain, Remove hence to yonder place; and it shall remove; and nothing shall be impossible to you" (Matthew 17:20).

The above verse has added to our understanding of how to get what we say by showing us that we only need *a little faith*; and once again, we see that we must *put that faith into words*. Once you understand what faith is, it is as easy to have the faith as it is to speak the words.

What is faith, anyway? First of all, I want to point out what faith is not: faith is not feelings. You can feel like something is going to happen, and it won't happen; but when you have faith that something is going to happen, it will.

Both the Old Testament and the New Testament speak of Abraham as an example to us of faith. "Abraham believed God, and it was imputed unto him for righteousness" (James 2:23). What did Abraham believe? When Abraham was in the prime of life, God had promised to give him a son, and had told Abraham that his descendents would be countless. Yet at ninety-nine, Abraham was still without an heir, when God appeared to him and told him that "my covenant will I establish with Isaac, which Sarah shall bear unto thee at this set time in the next year" (Genesis 17:21). The Bible reveals to us that this took *two* miracles, since both Sarah and Abraham were by that time too old to have children! Sarah's miracle was also by faith. Hebrews 11:11 tell us that "Through faith also Sarah herself received strength to conceive seed, and was delivered of a child when she was past age, because she judged him faithful who had promised."

The Bible tells us that Abraham, "being not weak in faith . . . considered not his own body now dead, when he was about an hundred years old, neither yet the deadness of Sarah's womb: He staggered not at the promise of God through unbelief; but was strong in faith, giving glory to God; And being fully persuaded that, what he had promised, he was able also to perform. And therefore it was imputed to him for righteousness" (Romans 4: 19-22).

From my own experiences, and from Scripture, I am convinced that Abraham didn't *feel* like he was able to father a son. In fact, the Bible records that when God told him the son was to be born the following year, "Then Abraham fell upon his face, and laughed, and said in his heart, Shall a child be born unto him that is an hundred years old? and shall Sarah, that is ninety years old, bear?" (Genesis 17:17).

Later—but before Isaac was born—Sarah heard God repeat His promise of a son to Abraham: "Now Abraham and Sarah were old and well stricken in age; and it ceased to be with Sarah after the manner of women. Therefore Sarah laughed within herself, saying, After I am waxed old shall I have pleasure, my lord being old also?" (Genesis 18:11-12). So we see that, although Scripture attributes the birth of Isaac to the faith of both Abraham and Sarah, neither Sarah nor Abraham *felt* like they were going to be parents. In fact, when God continued to promise Isaac's birth, both Abraham and Sarah laughed about it—which is why God told them to name the child Isaac, which means laughter.

When Abraham believed God, "it was imputed unto him for righteousness." Faith is pleasing to God, and "Without faith it is impossible to please him [God]: for he that cometh to God must believe that he is, and that he is a rewarder of them that diligently seek him" (Hebrews 11:6).

Since faith is such a crucial issue in our relationship to God, it's a good thing that it's a gift from Him (see Ephesians 2:8), and also that "God hath dealt to every man the measure of faith" (Romans 12:3). In fact, since God has dealt to every man a measure of faith—and all we need to move a mountain is a mustard seed's worth—we don't need to worry about whether we have faith or not. All we need to do is to decide to apply the faith we already have in the right direction.

I praise the Lord that faith doesn't depend on our feelings. After all, we can't decide how to feel. Generally speaking, feelings are something that happen to us, not something we decide in advance. But faith isn't a matter of emotions, or feelings, or even our physical senses. Faith is a matter of will. Since we already have "a measure of faith" (whether we feel as though we do or not), all we have to do to "have faith" is to decide to take God's Word for the matter in question.

If we decide to take God's Word for something (which shouldn't be hard to do: Titus 1:2 tells us God cannot lie) then we can *know* we have what God has promised us, even before we are able to see that thing come to pass. That is why the writer of Hebrews says, "Now faith is the substance of things hoped for, the evidence of things not seen" (Hebrews 11:1). If we decide to take God's Word for it, that very decision (faith) is the evidence to us that we will get the "things not seen" that we hoped for.

When my wife decided to take God's Word that the Lord was the strength of her life, she ached as much as ever. Her feet were still swollen. She had no evidence that she was healed—except the evidence of faith. She knew God's Word said, "The Lord is the strength of my life," so she knew she had strength. Since she had strength, she got up and walked—and after she got up and walked, she found that God's Word was true.

Now, in order to believe something without knowing it is true by the knowledge of our five senses, we have to have some other way of knowing it is true. (If we don't know it's true, then we can only hope it, we can't believe it.) The only way of doing this, of course, is that since God cannot lie, we know we can believe anything God says in His Word. If it is in God's Word, we can know that it's true. That is why Jesus said, "If ye abide in me, *and my words abide in you*, ye shall ask what ye will, and it shall be done unto you," (John 15:7; italics added).

What a promise! It's like a blank check on the bank of heaven: "ye shall ask what ye will, and it shall be done!" And the best part is that God's Word—which is thoroughly dependable—contains many of these all-inclusive promises, in addition to some very specific ones. Here are some more "blank checks" on God's Bank of Miracles:

"And whatsoever ye shall ask in my name, that will I do, that the Father may be glorified in the Son" (John 14:13).

"If ye shall ask any thing in my name, I will do it," (John 14:14).

"That whatsoever ye shall ask of the Father in my name, he may give it you" (John 15:16).

"Ask, and it shall be given you," (Matthew 7:7).

God's Word promises that if you are a believer, you have only to ask—and *What You Say Is What You Get!*

THE POWER OF "MERE" WORDS

If any man among you seem to be religious, and bridleth not his tongue, but deceiveth his own heart, this man's religion is vain (James 1:26).

For he that will love life, and see good days, let him refrain his tongue from evil, and his lips that they speak no guile (1 Peter 3:10).

A wholesome tongue is a tree of life: but perverseness therein is a breach in the Spirit (Proverbs 15:4).

Set a watch, O LORD, before my mouth; keep the door of my lips (Psalm 141:3).

Pleasant words are as an honeycomb, sweet to the soul, and health to the bones (Proverbs 16:24).

In the multitude of words there wanteth not sin: but he that restraineth his lips is wise (Proverbs 10:19).

The lips of the righteous feed many: but fools die for want of wisdom (Proverbs 10:21).

Whosoever therefore shall confess me before men, him will I confess also before my Father which is in heaven. But whosoever shall deny me before men, him will I also deny before my Father which is in heaven (Matthew 10:32-33).

I will give you a mouth and wisdom, which all your adversaries shall not be able to gainsay nor resist (Luke 21:15).

For with the heart man believeth unto righteousness; and with the mouth confession is made unto salvation (Romans 10:10).

Every idle word that men shall speak, they shall give account thereof in the day of judgment. For by thy words thou shalt be justified, and by thy words thou shalt be condemned (Matthew 12:36-37).

A man hath joy by the answer of his mouth: and a word spoken in due season, how good is it! (Proverbs 15:23).

The mouth of a righteous man is a well of life (Proverbs 10:11).

Whoso keepeth his mouth and his tongue, keepeth his soul from troubles (Proverbs 21:23).

Let no corrupt communication proceed out of your mouth, but that which is good to the use of edifying, that it may minister grace unto the hearers (Ephesians 4:29).

Chapter Four

CAN'T IS A FOUR-LETTER WORD

One of my jobs as a minister is, I believe, to pray for the sick. "Is any sick among you? Let him call for the elders of the church; and let them pray over him, anointing him with oil in the name of the Lord: And the prayer of faith shall save the sick, and the Lord shall raise him up; and if he have committed sins, they shall be forgiven him" (James 5:14-15). In spite of the fact, however, that the Bible promises healing for the sick, there was one woman in my early healing ministry who laid a particularly heavy burden on my heart. She was suffering from an extreme case of long-standing asthma. I had had to pray for her many times and each time she seemed no better.

She approached me one day to tell me about her troubles. Deeply sincere but discouraged to the point that she could not talk to me without crying, she said, "Brother Gossett, I don't understand why I can't receive healing. I know of other people for whom you have prayed, people who suffered from asthma, and they have been healed. If it is true that God is no respecter of persons, why doesn't He heal *me*?"

I answered, "I don't know why you have not received your healing, but go ahead and tell me all about yourself."

Immediately she began to pour out her heart. She told me all about her illness and the fact that she seemed unable to receive healing. "I have had this asthma for many years, but I can't be healed of it. I have been prayed for many times. Others besides you have prayed, but I just can't get healed. Some nights I have such a smothering attack of this asthma that I think I shall never be able to draw one more breath. The next day, after such an attack, I can't even get out of bed. At other times, I am all right at the beginning of the day, but by noon the asthma will have started up again, and I simply can't do anything. I work in an office, and many days I can't even finish my day's work because of my hard breathing and wheezing. I have prayed; I have fasted; I have searched my heart. *Why* can't I receive healing?"

I looked down at that woman. Everything about her showed her sincerity. She was obviously very earnest about seeking to receive her healing from the Lord.

"Mrs. Allison," I began, "I want to help you, and I believe that Jesus wants to heal you, but there is something that you must overcome, something just as serious as this asthma, before you can be healed of this asthma."

Her puzzled expression seemed to be saying to me, "I don't understand what you're talking about. I have tried *everything*."

I didn't even wait for her to put that question into words. I spoke directly to her and to her problem. "If I point out something that I feel is very important, can I be perfectly honest with you and give it to you straight? You know how much I want to help you. Will you take it from me, knowing that I am only the Lord's servant?"

Without a moment's hesitation, she replied, "Oh, yes, I have come to you for the truth, and I want you to *tell* me the truth. Help me in any way you can. If the Lord shows you anything about my life that is not as it should be, I want you to tell me. You won't hurt my feelings. Please tell me."

Quietly and slowly I explained to her: "It is true that you do have a serious case of asthma, but what I was referring to—something that is just as serious, if not more serious than the asthma—is your negative attitude. You have as bad a case of 'I-can't-itis' as I have ever witnessed. I have been listening to you, and no fewer than a dozen times you have said, 'I can't. I can't be healed. I can't get my breath. I can't get out of bed in the morning. I can't continue in the day. I can't stay at the office.' Your life seems to be made up of 'I can't' do this and 'I can't' do that. Now, nowhere in the Bible does God describe you as an 'I-can't-er.' But somehow you have taken on this malady of 'I-can't-itis.' Before you can expect any improvement in your life, any healing, you just must change that 'I can't' to 'I can.' Until you do that, God cannot move to help you as He wishes to do."

The entire time I had been talking to her, she had been crying. As moved as I was about her trouble and her emotional condition, I knew that I must continue, if I were to help her to open the door to God and His grace and His power.

She accepted my comments and, still crying, she asked through her tears, "But what can I do about it? How can I change my attitude?"

I opened my Bible to Philippians 4:13; I handed it to her and asked her to read what it said. Softly but with a determination that I had not heard in her voice before, she read, "I can do all things through Christ which strengtheneth me."

"Now, *that's* the secret," I told her. "Instead of saying, 'I *can't* receive healing,' begin to affirm: 'Through Christ who strengthens me, I *can* do all things; I *can* receive healing; I *can* be made completely whole through Christ, Who is my strength and my healer; by His stripes I am healed.'"

It was not an instant recovery. Mrs. Allison had practiced "I can't" so long that it required real discipline for her to train her unruly lips to speak God's Word. Many months later, however, I saw her again. This time she was joyful and bright. She eagerly shared with me her testimony of God's complete healing of the painful, frightening asthma that had so long plagued her life.

Now I want to give you an "instant replay" of what Mrs. Allison was saying before she learned how to receive her healing: "I have had this asthma for many years, but *I can't be healed of it.* I have been prayed for many times. Others beside you have prayed, but *I just can't get healed.*"

What Mrs. Allison said was what Mrs. Allison got. When she said, "I just can't get healed," she couldn't get healed. When she said, "I can be made completely whole through Christ, Who is my strength and my healer, and by His stripes I am healed," then she was healed. Granted, it was not an instant recovery. Even people who have practiced building up their faith for years do not always get *instant* recoveries. But the point is, *she got healed.* Not only did Mrs. Allison *own* her healing, in the sense that she had God's written Word that "with his stripes we are healed," (Isaiah 53:5), but in time she also *took possession of* her healing, in that she no longer had to *believe* for a healing because she could *feel* her healing with every breath she drew.

What You Say Is What You Get.

AGREEING WITH GOD

"Can two walk together, except they be agreed?" (Amos 3:3).

"Enoch walked with God" (Genesis 5:24).

1.   Many people desire to walk with God. But how can we truly walk with God, unless we agree with God? To agree with God is to say the same thing God says in His Word about salvation, healing, answers to prayer, and everything else He tells us. We must know that God cannot lie, and that since he cannot lie, everything He tells us must be true—so it should be easy for us to be able to agree with it. The Bible calls agreeing with God "having faith."

> By faith Enoch was translated that he should not see death; and was not found, because God had translated him: for before his translation he had this testimony, that he pleased God. But without faith it is impossible to please him: for he that cometh to God must believe that he is, and that he is a rewarder of them that diligently seek him. (Hebrews 11:5-6)

2.   We must agree with God that *we are who God says we are:* His heaven-born children, new creatures in Christ, more than conquerors through Christ. We must disagree with the

devil, who tries to tell us we are "no good," "a failure," "a weakling," "a bad Christian." We have to *agree with God* and *disagree with the devil* in order to walk with God.

3.   We must agree with God that *we have what He says we have:* His name, His nature, His power, His authority, His love. Through His Word, we own these things already—but we must take possession of them by our spoken words. We possess what we confess. Like Joshua and Caleb, we are the rightful owners of what God has already given us in His Word—but we have to take possession of our "promised land" by faith.

4.   Enoch walked with God—and so do we, by agreeing that *God has given us the ability to do what God says we can do:* witness with power, cast out demons, lay hands on the sick and have them recover. We "can do all things through Christ."

5.   If we speak only what our senses dictate, or what the doctor (or accountant, or scientist, or whoever) tells us, then we will not agree with God. It is by speaking "the Word only" that we agree with God. It is "a good confession" of faith that is our victory.

6.   In order to walk with God, we must disagree with the devil. Jesus did this by boldly

declaring, "It is written" when He was tempted in the wilderness. (See Matthew 4 and Luke 4.) We, too, must resist the devil by the Word.

7. Daily, we must walk with God by agreeing with God and His Word. Because "he hath said...so that we may boldly say" (Hebrews 13:5-6).

Chapter Five

IS SILENCE GOLDEN?

People say that silence is golden, and it certainly is true that it can be very expensive. I know of more than one case in which silence has cost a person the thing they wanted most from God.

One morning I prayed for a sick woman. Both of us were overjoyed at the result: she felt perfectly well. Not long after that, she called me to come see her again.

"I am so disturbed. My symptoms are back, just as bad as ever. I can't understand what's wrong," she confessed to me.

"When your husband came home last night, did you tell him you were healed?" I asked. I could readily feel her faltering and wavering, her indecision.

"No," she defended herself. "You see, I wasn't *sure* yet. I didn't want to say anything until I was positive."

"But you had no pain," I responded. "Was there any soreness?"

"Oh, no, that had all left," she agreed. "But, you see, I have to be very careful. My husband is a skeptic, and I didn't want to tell him until I was sure."

This woman lost her fight because she doubted the Word. Had she dared to stand her ground on the Word and had held fast to her confession that she was healed, she would have reaped positive results. God promises in Jeremiah 1:12 ". . . I will hasten my word to perform it."

One of my close friends is T.L. Osborn, the world-famous missionary and evangelist. One day, we spent five whole hours just talking about truth and the power of the confession of God's Word.

Osborn started the conversation when he told me, "This Bible truth of the effect of the confession of the Word has been the great springboard to my whole ministry around the world." Then, as we finally ended our discussion that unforgettable day, his final words to me were, "Don, knowing what you do about the confession of the Word makes you a man richly blessed by God."

He was right. Since I have come to understand the importance of what I say—since I have learned what to say and also what not to say—my life has been blessed beyond anything I could have dreamed of asking for. Unfortunately, in our society the word "confession" has come to have mainly a negative, rather than a positive, meaning. Today we usually associate confession with guilt. People who have committed crimes "confess" them. And some denominations stress negative confessions: confessions of sins, faults, shortcomings, weaknesses, and failures.

Even according to most dictionary definitions, confession carries with it the idea of guilt. But the definition that Christians can claim, one which is also in the secular dictionary, is "the acknowledgment of a belief." For followers of Jesus, that means the acknowledgment of His saving power. It includes Jesus' promise to confess *us* before God if we overcome the testings of this world. Revelation 3:5 tells us that "He that overcometh, the same shall be clothed in white raiment; and I will not blot out his name out of the book of life, but I will confess his name before my Father, and before His angels." There is no wavering in those words. There is no indecision. Jesus said, "I will confess his name before His angels." When Jesus confesses our name before the Father, we will be allowed to rule with Him in the life to come. "To him that overcometh will I grant to sit with me in my throne" (Revelation 3:21). "Whosoever therefore shall confess me before men, him will I confess also before my Father which is in heaven" (Matthew 10:32).

This is not to say that there is no place for the kind of confession we associate with admitting guilt or acknowledging our sins to God. In both 1 John 1:9 and James 5:16 are found directives to do just that in order to get right with God and to continue in fellowship with Him and with our fellow-men.

The confession of our faith (as opposed to the confession of our sins) is the confession of God's Word. Hearing God's Word, claiming it for your own, saying His promise is for you, and receiving the results of that promise are the orderly and direct steps along the pathway to God. Fortunately for us, however, God does not wait until we have gone through all those steps, as if we were working for some kind of permit, license, or diploma. At our very first turning toward Him, like a father, He stretches out His hand and draws us steadfastly along the way. While we are still in the babyhood of faith, He is urging us toward that positive confession of His place in every area of our lives. He will never draw away from *us*. If we falter or waver, however, He gives us back the choice, and we may lose ground in our spiritual progress.

What you confess, you possess. If it is a negative confession, the results will be negative. If it is a positive confession, the results will be Godward. Many people spoil their confession by wavering between the positive "Yes" and the faltering "No." James said, "let him ask in faith, nothing wavering. For he that wavereth is like a wave of the sea driven with the wind and tossed. For let not that man think that he shall receive any thing of the Lord" (James 1:6,7). When your heart gives a ringing positive "Yes" to the Word, positive results will begin to occur in your life.

I POSSESS WHAT I CONFESS

I know what I confess and I know what I possess.

I confess Jesus as my Lord (Romans 10:9-10); *I possess* salvation.

I confess that "with his stripes we are healed" (Isaiah 53:5); *I possess* healing.

I confess that the Son has made me free (John 8:36); *I possess* absolute freedom.

I confess that "the love of God is shed abroad in our hearts by the Holy Ghost" (Romans 5:5); *I possess* the ability to love everyone.

I confess that "the righteous are bold as a lion" (Proverbs 28:1); *I possess* lion-hearted boldness in spiritual warfare against the devil.

I confess that "he hath said, I will never leave thee nor forsake thee" (Hebrews 13:5); *I possess* the presence of God each step of my way.

I confess that I am "the redeemed of the Lord" (Psalm 107:2); *I possess* redemption benefits every day.

I confess that the anointing of the Holy One abideth in me (1 John 2:27); *I possess* yoke-destroying results by His anointing.

I confess that in the name of Jesus I can cast out devils (Mark 16:17); *I possess* the authority for dynamic deliverances.

I confess that I can lay my hands on the sick and they will recover (Mark 16:18); *I possess* healing power for those oppressed by sickness.

I confess that my God shall supply all of my needs (Philippians 4:19); I will lack for nothing since *I possess* God's abundant supply.

Confess and possess. The way is clearly marked.

Chapter Six

HONESTY IS THE BEST POLICY

Herod Antipas ruled over Galilee from the time Jesus was a little boy until 39 A.D., and he was a bad guy if there ever was one. He came by his wickedness naturally, since his father, Herod the Great, was the Herod who slaughtered all the Jewish boys under two years of age when he heard that Jesus had been born. But Herod Antipas did a number of bad things on his own account: he married his brother's wife; he had John the Baptist killed; he killed James the brother of John; and he had Peter cast into prison, intending to kill him. (Peter escaped.) Finally, however, Herod did something *so* wicked that God killed him for it. What do you think it was? The Bible says,

> And upon a set day Herod, arrayed in royal apparel, sat upon his throne, and made an oration... And the people gave a shout, saying, It is the voice of a god, and not of a

man. And immediately the angel of the Lord smote him, *because he gave not God the glory*: and he was eaten of worms, and gave up the ghost. But the word of God grew and multiplied. [Acts 12:21-24; italics added]

If you are going to go on with God and learn to "Heal the sick, cleanse the lepers, raise the dead, cast out devils" (Matthew 10:8), then there is one vitally important principle to keep in mind: you need to remember to give God the glory. "Every good gift and every perfect gift is from above, and cometh down from the Father" (James 1:17). If you have a powerful gift of healing, or if you are in a position of great authority, it is only because God gave you that gift; He placed you where you are. The Bible teaches us that "there is no power but of God: the powers that be are ordained of God" (Romans 13:1). Everything you have, you have because God gave it to you.

Herod Antipas wasn't the only king in the Bible to forget where his power came from: Nebuchadnezzar was another. In the book of Daniel, Nebuchadnezzar has recorded his story as a testimony "unto all people, nations, and languages, that dwell in the earth." Nebuchadnezzar tells us that he:

Walked in the palace of the kingdom of Babylon. The king spake, and said, Is not this great Babylon, that I have built for the house of the kingdom by the might of my power, and for the honour of my majesty? While the word was in the king's mouth, there fell a voice from heaven, saying, O king Nebuchadnezzar, to thee it is spoken; The kingdom is departed from thee. And they shall drive thee from men, and thy dwelling shall be with the beasts of the field: they shall make thee to eat grass as oxen, and seven times shall pass over thee, until thou know that the most High ruleth in the kingdom of men, and giveth it to whomsoever he will. The same hour was the thing fulfilled upon Nebuchadnezzar; and he was driven from men, and did eat grass as oxen, and his body was wet with the dew of heaven, till his hairs were grown like eagles' feathers, and his nails like birds' claws. And at the end of the days I Nebuchadnezzar lifted up mine eyes unto heaven, and mine understanding returned unto me, and I blessed the most High, and I praised and honoured him that liveth for ever, whose dominion is an everlasting dominion, and his kingdom is from generation to generation. . . . At the same time my reason returned unto me . . . and I was established in my kingdom, and excellent majesty was added unto me. Now I Nebuchadnezzar praise and extol and honour the King of heaven, all whose works are truth, and his ways judgment: and those that walk in pride he is able to abase. [Daniel 4:29-37]

Do you begin to see how jealous God is for His glory? And do you begin to see how dangerous it is to take His glory—glory for something He has done—and give yourself the credit for something He has done for you?

Nebuchadnezzar said that *he* had built his kingdom by the might of *his* power, and for the honour of *his* majesty, and while the words were still in his mouth, the kingdom was taken from him. He was insane for seven years until he learned to give God the glory.

Herod's misdeed was a little more serious: he actually allowed people to worship him. For that, he got the death penalty.

Barnabas and Paul ran into this kind of dangerous situation in Lystra, where Paul healed a cripple. When the people saw what Paul had done they said, "The gods are come down to us in the likeness of men" (Acts 14:11), and they prepared to do sacrifice to Paul and Barnabas. When Paul and Barnabas heard of this, they tore their clothes as a sign of distress and ran among the people, saying, "Sirs, why do ye these things? We also are men of like passions with you, and preach unto you that ye should turn from these vanities unto the living God ... And with these sayings scarce restrained they the people, that they had not done sacrifice unto them" (Acts 14:15, 18).

Paul and Barnabas weren't about to let people give them the glory that belonged to God alone. As they told the crowd, they were nobody special—they were men "of like passions" with the idol-worshippers in Lystra. They had the power of God, but it was God's power, not their power. It's important to understand that *What You Say Is What You Get*, not because your words themselves have power, but because your own words make it possible for God's power to work on your behalf.

If your words had their own power—and something happened because you said it would—that would be "mind over matter." I don't believe in "mind over matter." The Bible says that the disciples "went forth, and preached everywhere, the Lord working with them, and confirming the word with signs following" (Mark 16:20). Jesus said, "If ye ask anything in my name, I will do it" (John 14:14). Who does the work? Jesus does the work. You do the asking, and Jesus does the giving. You do the preaching, and Jesus confirms the word. You say—and Jesus does. Since God does all the work, it's important to give Him all the glory for it. If you don't, He has ways of showing you—as He showed Nebuchadnezzar—that He's in charge. Christians must be fanatically honest. They must not claim for themselves the glory that belongs to God.

When I preach the message that *What You Say Is What You Get*, there are two basic misunderstandings that keep recurring: one is the one I've just dealt with—some people think I preach "mind over matter" instead of "God over everything." The other misunderstanding is nearly as bad: When I preach that if God's Word says you're healed, then you *are* healed, some people take that as a license to say anything at all, just as long as it's positive—*even if it isn't true!*

If you fall down the stairs, and your ankle is black and blue and extremely sore and swollen, what are you supposed to say about it? You *can* say, "I believe I'm healed," because God's Word says, "with his stripes we are healed" (Isaiah 53:5). God can't lie. If He says you are healed, then you are healed. You can believe what God says. You can say what God says. But you *can't* say your ankle isn't swollen, black and blue, and sore. The Holy Spirit is the spirit of Truth. Jesus said, "the hour cometh, and now is, when the true worshippers shall worship the Father in spirit and in truth: for the Father seeketh such to worship him" (John 4:23).

In a Walt Disney story entitled *Bambi*, a mother deer says to her fawn, "If you can't say anything good, don't say anything at all." It's not Scripture, but there's a lot of truth in what that mother deer is supposed to have said. If you can't say anything true, at least you don't have to lie. If you can't say anything positive, you can at least keep your mouth shut. Until you learn how to make a positive confession, you don't *have* to say anything. "A fool uttereth all his mind, but a wise man keepeth it in till afterwards" (Proverbs 29:11).

Well, what *should* you do during the waiting period between what you say and what you get? If your ankle is sore, you can say, "I am healed because God's Word says I am healed." Or you can say, "My ankle hurts, but I believe I'm healed because God's Word says I'm healed and God's Word can't lie." Or you can say, "I'm not looking to the way my ankle feels, I'm looking to what God's Word says about it, and God's Word says it's healed." Obviously, you can't say your ankle doesn't hurt if it does hurt. So since you can't say it doesn't hurt, you don't need to say anything at all about it (other than that God's Word says it's healed), unless someone insists on hearing how it feels. God doesn't want us to lie about anything, no matter what our motives are. "The word of the Lord is right; and all his works are done in truth" (Psalm 33:4).

SAY WHAT GOD SAYS

Some people have a problem confessing that they have a thing by faith before they can see—or feel—that they already have the thing that they are asking for. They're afraid that they might be telling lies. But since God cannot lie, we also cannot lie whenever we *say what God says*.

I. We Are Who God Says We Are

We are new creatures: "if any man be in Christ, he is a new creature: old things are passed away; behold, all things are become new" (2 Corinthians 5:17).

We are "delivered . . . from the power of darkness" (Colossians 1:13).

"We are more than conquerors through him that loved us" (Romans 8:37).

We are "heirs of God, and joint-heirs with Christ" (Romans 8:17).

We are "blessed . . . with all spiritual blessings . . . in Christ" (Ephesians 1:3).

II. We Have What God Says We Have

We have life: "He that hath the Son hath life; he that hath not the Son of God hath not life" (1 John 5:12).

We have light: "He that followeth me shall not walk in darkness, but shall have the light of life" (John 8:12).

We have liberty: "Where the Spirit of the

Lord is, there is liberty" (2 Corinthians 3:17).

We have love: "The love of God is shed abroad in our hearts" (Romans 5:5).

We have joy: "Your joy no man taketh from you" (John 16:22).

We have pardon: "The blood of Jesus Christ his Son cleanseth us from all sin (1 John 1:7).

We have peace: "We have peace with God through our Lord Jesus Christ" (Romans 5:1).

We have purpose: "For me to live is Christ" (Philippians 1:21).

We have power: "Ye shall receive power, after that the Holy Ghost is come upon you" (Acts 1:8).

We have provision: "My God shall supply all your need" (Philippians 4:19).

We have prospect: "In my Father's house are many mansions...I go to prepare a place for you" (John 14:2).

III. We Can Do What God Says We Can Do

We can "do all things through Christ" (Philippians 4:13). We can cast out demons and minister healing to the sick. (Mark 16:17-18). We can share with the world what we have in Christ!

Affirm these words, "I am who God says I am. I have what God says I have. I can do what God says I can do."

Chapter Seven

HOW TO MULTIPLY YOUR MONEY

At the close of a radio service I had been conducting recently, a young woman in Vancouver, British Columbia, came to talk with me. She had come to Vancouver from Saskatchewan, where she had been born and raised.

"All of my life I have known poverty," she stated. "My family and all the people I knew and grew up with were poor. Now, here in Vancouver, it seems that the same thing is true. My friends and acquaintances are poor. They have hardly an extra dollar for anything. There is so much that I would love to do for the Lord, but it really takes all that I have just to buy the necessities for my son and myself. I am bound by poverty, but I just believe that somehow God has an answer for me."

"I'm glad to hear you talking this way," I answered. "I, too, am convinced that God has the answer to poverty. I remember how very poor my own family was back during the depression years. When my mother recently visited me, she reminded me that we were so poor that when our clock broke beyond repair, we couldn't afford to buy a new one! In our home there was never enough milk to have a second bowl of cereal for breakfast. If you wanted a second bowl of cereal, you had to save the milk from your first bowl—or eat your corn flakes dry. I *know* firsthand what it's like to be poor and unable to pay your bills. I too hate poverty, and I am convinced that I have found God's answer for it."

The faith in this young woman's voice stimulated me. I'm convinced she's on the road to overcoming poverty. As I thought of her statements to me and recalled my own early poverty-stricken home, I just wanted to reach out to help every Christian understand God's plan of prosperity.

God has a divine law of giving and receiving. If you want to receive financial help from God, you need to understand that it is the measure with which you give that determines what you will receive from God. The more you give, the more you get: God always sees to it that you get more than you give. Jesus said, "Give, and it shall be given unto you; good measure, pressed down, and shaken together, and running over, shall men give into your bosom. For with the same measure that you mete withal it shall be measured to you again" (Luke 6:38).

If you are not getting your prayers answered, you should take stock of the matter of your giving— particularly if it is especially your prayers about finances that seem to go unheard. God's Word says that withholding your tithes and offerings is tantamount to robbing God:

> Will a man rob God? Yet ye have robbed me. But ye say, Wherein have we robbed thee? In tithes and offerings. Ye are cursed with a curse: for ye have robbed me, even this whole nation. Bring ye all the tithes into the storehouse, that there may be meat in mine house, and prove me now herewith, saith the LORD of hosts, if I will not open you the windows of heaven, and pour you out a blessing, that there shall not be room enough to receive it. And I will rebuke the devourer for your sakes. [Malachi 3:8-11]

If you rob God of tithes and offerings, you are the loser in the long run. God says it emphatically, "Ye are cursed with a curse, for ye have robbed me of tithes and offerings."

Tithing (giving one-tenth of your gross income to God) is a hard step of faith for many new Christians, but it is a step with which God commands us to prove him. Besides tithes, Malachi says, we also owe God offerings. An offering is anything you give God *over and above* a tenth of your gross income.

Paying your tithes and offerings may seem like a hard thing to do at first, until you realize God's reason for asking you to do it. His reason for asking you to give to Him is so that He may give to you. God has bound Himself to give to people as they give to Him. If they give liberally, He will give liberally; if they are stingy with Him, He will be stingy with them. But God will give back whatever is given to

Him "pressed down, shaken together, and running over." He will "open the windows of heaven, and pour out a blessing, that there shall not be room enough to contain it." Furthermore, God promises to rebuke the devourer for your sakes.

Wouldn't you like to have God's protection from unexpected and unnecessary financial calamities? You will—*if* you pay Him what you owe Him. If not, you will be like the people God spoke to in Haggai, who had been withholding tithes:

> Ye have sown much, and bring in little; ye eat, but ye have not enough; ye drink, but ye are not filled with drink; ye clothe you, but there is none warm; *and he that earneth wages earneth wages to put it into a bag with holes.* [Haggai 1:6; italics added]

If you have been robbing God of tithes and offerings, don't go on with the firm disapproval of God upon your life. Pay up your tithes, give your offerings in the Lord's name, and know that God will do for you what He says He will. He will open for you the windows of heaven, pour you out an overflowing blessing, and will rebuke the devourer for your sake! This is one place in Scripture that God actually invites us to prove Him.

Paying your tithes and giving your offerings are the only scriptural ways that God promises to open for you the windows of heaven. Some of you are dry, barren and empty in your spiritual lives because you have been stingy with God. You are paying for your disobedience in spiritual leanness!

Someone will ask, "Do you mean that I have to buy the blessings of God by paying tithes and giving offerings?" Absolutely not. Money can't buy anything from God. But when you pay your tithe and give your offerings, you are *cooperating with your Creator*. God has said in His Word that He will be liberal to those who are liberal, and stingy to those who are stingy. *He can't go back on His Word!*

Withholding from God tends to poverty, the Bible tells us. God wants to produce tremendous blessings for you, spiritually, physically and financially. Thousands testify to this fact. Real giving is an act of faith. Failure to give is unbelief. It is giving place to the devil. I charge you: resist the devil and he will flee. Tell him he's a liar. Believe God's Word and be blessed. Listen to the devil's doubts and you will lose the financial blessing God wants to give to you.

I dare you to do something great in the realm of giving. God gives you a great challenge. He says, "Prove me now herewith, saith the Lord, with your tithes and offerings, and see if I will not open for you the windows of heaven, and pour you a blessing that there shall not be room enough to receive it, and I will rebuke the devourer for your sakes!" God simply says, "Prove me."

I know a lady who was experiencing poverty. She had only enough money to pay her fuel bill, when she accepted God's challenge to "prove Him" with her money. Do you know what God did for her? He caused five times more money than she had given to come to her from unexpected sources, all because she dared to take God at His Word.

If you are experiencing poverty, you can *give your way to prosperity*. If you are poverty-stricken you can't do anything better than to give boldly to God!

The matter of giving is simply a matter of whether you believe the Bible or not. People who do believe the Bible on giving obtain great blessings from God. I am zealous for you to have God's best. Search out the powerful promises of the Bible on giving. Then act on God's Word.

Remember that God is not a man that He should lie. And God has promised that He "will pour you out a blessing (spiritual and financial) that there shall not be room enough to receive" if you will prove Him with your tithes and offerings. This is called a "prove God" offering.

I remember when I gave my first "prove God" offering. My wife and I were travelling from Chillicothe, Missouri, where we had just closed an evangelistic campaign and stopped off at Carthage, Missouri, to visit the meetings being conducted by Evangelist Jack Coe.

Our car payment for the 1947 Ford we drove had taken almost all our money.

One night Brother Coe received what he called a "Prove Me" offering. He based the offering upon Malachi 3:8-11, the passage I quoted to you earlier.

Over and over Brother Coe emphasized the fact that this was the Word of God, not the word of man. This was God's challenge. God was warning His people to cease robbing Him by withholding tithes and offerings.

As Brother Coe read these words, suddenly it seemed that he was not speaking, but that God was speaking through his lips.

I needed to prove God. I needed to have God open heaven's windows unto my life. I desired blessings which I would not be able to contain.

And I desperately needed to have God rebuke the devourer (Satan) for my sake.

I investigated my ability to give. In my wallet I had one dollar. In my pocket I had a nickel. I knew my wife had nothing. There was nothing in the bank. Nor was there any money hidden away elsewhere. That was it. My total finances were one dollar and five cents.

In order to make the step more real and personal, Brother Coe invited everyone to bring their "prove God" offerings up to the front, and lay them right on the Bible, which he had left opened at Malachi 3.

I knew God was challenging me to do something that seemed totally unreasonable. My wife was expecting our first baby. I thought: what if she should need something special? Or what if I had some unexpected car expense?

I tried to figure an "out" in case this didn't work, but I knew it was carnal reasoning. I knew that if I allowed it to persist I would quench and grieve the Holy Spirit. I believe that many people miss God's best in the realm of Spirit-led giving because they resort to carnal reasoning, thereby quenching, resisting, and grieving the Spirit.

I could hear Brother Coe's words again, "Prove me, saith the Lord, and I will open the windows of heaven unto you. I will pour out upon you an overflowing blessing. I will rebuke Satan's work of poverty from your life. And ye shall be delightsome, saith the Lord."

I was only twenty-one years old. This was a new experience for me. Yet I could see I was clearly hearing the Word of God. I had trusted His Word as the sole basis of my salvation. I had claimed everlasting life on the basis of His Word. I had staked my whole life on His Word, in accepting His holy call to preach the Gospel.

Why couldn't I trust His Word in giving?

I looked at my dear wife seated next to me. I looked again inside my wallet at that lonely dollar bill.

What should I do? My delay gave the devil an opportunity to move in with a few of his subtle doubts. Cunningly he whispered to me, "This is foolish. You can't afford to give that dollar. Think of your wife. Think of your car. An emergency might arise. Don't listen to that preacher. Others have more money than you do. Let *them* give. Hang on to that last dollar of yours."

By this time, I knew this was the voice of the deceiver, the devil. I had already learned that one of his most deceitful devices is to instill the thought in people's minds that "others will do it."

Besides, I knew that *God wanted me to give.* The Christian has a need to give. Giving is one of the most wonderful spiritual experiences to be discovered in the Christian life.

Remember the words of the Lord Jesus, how he said, "It is more blessed to give than to receive" (Acts 20:35).

Yes, there is a tremendous blessing in giving. Those who have discovered this fact know the importance of obeying the voice of the Spirit, when it comes to giving.

Suddenly I arose from my seat and marched down to the front to place my last dollar on the Bible, as my "Prove God" offering.

When I let go of that dollar, and placed it down on God's Word, I was excited! I knew I had obeyed God. I was cooperating with my Creator in something big and wonderful. God and I had gone into partnership.

I walked back to my seat with a spring in my step. I even felt lighter because I had given that last dollar!

I drove from that service to the home of some friends who had invited us to stay with them. I was singing praise choruses all the way to their home.

I had thought that possibly my sleep might be interrupted with money worries. Not so! I had given. I had committed the matter into God's loving hands. My life, my finances, and my responsibilities were really all His, anyway. So I rested in peace.

When I awakened early the next morning, the Spirit of God was moving within my heart! God had opened heaven's windows to my soul, and I was drinking in His spiritual blessing. Even if I had never received any financial blessings from that offering, the spiritual blessings would have been worth it all.

"Thou wilt shew me the path of life: in thy presence is fullness of joy; at thy right hand there are pleasures for evermore" (Psalm 16:11). Money can't buy happiness, much less joy. God's blessings are priceless.

Later that morning, I walked to the post office to

call for my mail. En route I met a Christian businessman whom I knew.

After greeting me there on the sidewalk, he looked earnestly at me and asked, "Don, how are you coming along?"

"Oh, just fine, thank you," I replied.

"Tell me: how are you coming along financially?" he asked.

"Oh, the Lord is good to us," I told him.

The Lord *was* good to us. We don't measure His goodness by how much money we have. No! The blessings of the Lord make rich and add no sorrow!

Then my friend said, "Well, you know I just feel impressed that I should do something to help you out in your good ministry for the Lord."

With that statement, he reached into his pocket to pull out his wallet. Nothing like this had ever happened to me, and I felt somewhat embarrassed. I looked up at the sky to avoid the appearance of being eager or inquisitive about what he was getting from his wallet.

When the man turned around to face me again, he grabbed my hand, and pressed a bill into it. I kept my hand tightly closed around that bill, for this was part of the miracle God had promised me the night before when I "proved God" by my giving. I thanked him for this gift, and we bade farewell.

He was walking in one direction, and I was going in the other. I kept peeking over my shoulder to see when he was far enough away from me so that he wouldn't see me opening my hand to discover what was inside.

(I told my wife later that I just knew it was more

than one dollar. It just "felt" like it was more than that! Besides, I *expected* it to be more than one dollar, for one dollar is the amount I gave. And God promised to give me a blessing too big to contain.)

When finally the friend was far enough away I opened up my hand, and there was a ten dollar bill! That was the biggest ten dollar bill I have ever seen! Not in size: it was standard in measurements. But because it was heaven-sent, to me it looked like a hundred dollars!

I actually forgot about my trip to the post office! I nearly ran back to where my wife was, to share with her the fact that God had already restored ten times the amount I had given the night before!

That same afternoon, I was scheduled to speak at a minister's meeting. It was clearly understood that since it was a minister's meeting, there would be no financial remuneration for my preaching there.

But just before I spoke, the leader of that fellowship of ministers, Brother Gilchrist, stood up and spoke to the brethren with deep emotion.

"Brethren, as you know it is not our policy to receive offerings for any of our speakers. We just never do. But today as I sat here on this platform, the Lord has spoken to my heart. The Lord has said we should receive an offering for Brother Don Gossett, who is going to speak to us this afternoon. I want everyone to obey the Lord, and we shall receive this special offering for Brother Gossett."

I was rejoicing inside, and I thought, "Hallelujah, God can change long-standing rules and procedures, if need be, to meet His servants' needs."

Those dear brethren gave me twenty-five dollars.

I knew this was God's way of responding to my step of faith the previous night, when I dared to "prove God" with my last dollar.

That was not the end. Ever since then, as I have continued to give, God has continued to bless us spiritually, physically, and financially in a wonderful way. It took several years for us to learn how to trust Him fully, but how glad I am that I made a start that day! I was glad at the time, as well. The knowledge I had laid up treasures in heaven, the assurance that I had obeyed the Lord—these were enough reward in themselves. But then God really did what He had said He would do. He opened up heaven's windows. He poured out upon me an overflowing blessing. He rebuked the devourer for my sake. And He made me glad.

WHAT TO EXPECT
AFTER YOU GIVE

Make this a personal affirmation of God's Word. God will do what He says.

1. I have proven God with tithes and offerings according to Malachi 3, and I now know that God will open the windows of heaven unto me, and pour out an overflowing blessing that there will not be room enough to receive. I am praising Him for opening heaven's windows to my soul and for His abundant blessing that makes rich and adds no sorrow.

2. Further, I know God has promised, in response to my loving obedience in giving, that He will rebuke the devourer for my sake. The devil is the devourer who would devour my finances, the harmony of my home, my peace of mind. I praise the Lord that He is rebuking the devourer for my sake!

3. I know that God is supplying all of my needs according to His riches in glory by Christ Jesus. I shall hold fast to this confession without wavering. James 1:7 declares that men who waver will not receive anything from the Lord. But I will not waver in my expectations that God will open heaven's windows, pouring out the blessings that there will not be room

enough to receive, and that He's rebuking the devourer for my sake. It is being done, hallelujah!

4. I have sown bountifully, so God declares that I shall reap bountifully. Bountiful blessings financially are mine, because God says so, and God is not a man that He should lie.

5. I have given not grudgingly nor of necessity, I have given cheerfully because "God loveth a cheerful giver" (2 Corinthians 9:7). I know that if I were to withhold from God that it would tend to poverty (Proverbs 11:24). But I practice liberality in my giving and thereby He ministers to all my needs.

6. I am discovering the reality of the words of Jesus that it is more blessed to give than to receive (Acts 20:35). To be a cheerful, hilarious giver (2 Corinthians 9:7) is the source of tremendous blessing, even greater than receiving. But as I give, the Lord just sees to it that it's given unto me, good measure, pressed down, and shaken together and running over shall men given unto my bosom (see Luke 6:38).

7. God's Word is His great "anti-poverty plan," to keep me in abundance of money and material possessions, to meet the needs of my family, and most of all, to give to the advancing of His Gospel world-wide.

Chapter Eight

MORE ABOUT MONEY

"The *love* of money is the root of all evil" (1 Timothy 6:10; italics added). It is not the money which is evil, but the *love* of money which can do us in. Jesus said, "How hard it is for them that trust in riches to enter the Kingdom of God" (Mark 10:24). When we love money more than God—when we trust money more than we trust God—we're in trouble. We lose out on a chance to let God bless us financially in this life, and we may lose out on going to heaven in the next.

Jesus said, "Whosoever will come after me, let him deny himself, and take up his cross, and follow me. For whosoever will save his life shall lose it; but whosoever shall lose his life for my sake and the gospel's, the same shall save it. For what shall it profit a man, if he shall gain the whole world, and lose his own soul?" (Mark 8:34-36). A man's soul, Jesus said, is worth more to that man than the entire world—and to save it, he must come to the point where he is willing to give up everything to follow God. Jesus put this transaction in terms of a balance sheet: profit *versus* loss.

The profit to be gained from doing God's will is more than just spiritual, although the spiritual gains to be made from obedience to God are of the utmost importance. But the Bible tells us that there is also a dollars-and-cents blessing to be realized from following God. Did you know that God pays interest? To those of us who, like Peter, have left all to follow Him, He pays interest of *ten thousand percent*! Jesus said, "There is no man that hath left house, or brethren, or sisters, or father, or mother, or wife, or children, or lands, for my sake, and the gospel's, But he shall receive an hundredfold now in this time, houses, and brethren, and sisters, and mothers, and children, and lands, with persecutions; and in the world to come eternal life" (Mark 10:29-30).

God knows our motives. If we give to get, He will still give back "shaken together, pressed down, and running over," but if we give for His sake, the interest rate is even higher: it's "an hundredfold!"

One of the reasons God wants us to give—especially our tithes and offerings—is so that we can keep money in its proper perspective. He wants money to have its proper place in our lives.

Improperly handled, *money can become our master*. We can become so bound by worry over how to get it and fear of losing it that it can keep us from doing the things God wants us to do and being the people God wants us to be. "No man can serve two masters," Jesus said, "for either he will hate the one and love the other; or else he will hold to the one, and despise the other. Ye cannot serve God and mammon. . . . Therefore take no thought, saying, what shall we eat? or, What shall we drink? or, Wherewithal shall we be clothed? . . . for your heavenly Father knoweth that ye have need of all these things. But seek ye first the kingdom of God, and his righteousness, and all these things shall be added unto you" (Matthew 6:24, 31-33).

In the above passage from the Sermon on the Mount, Jesus told the multitude that they could not serve money and God, but that if they would put God first, He would meet all their needs. *If God has not been meeting your needs, perhaps you have not been putting Him first.*

The Bible mentions three specific ways of not putting God first which are hindrances to financial prosperity. Left unchecked, these faults can nullify the principles I shared with you in Chapter Seven— and believe me, those principles *will* multiply your money if properly practiced, and if none of these hindrances are allowed to interfere.

The first of these hindrances to prosperity is as follows: "Take heed that ye do not your alms before men, to be seen of them: otherwise ye have no reward of your Father which is in heaven. . . . do not sound a trumpet before thee, as the hypocrites do . . . that they may have glory of men. Verily I say unto you, They have their reward. But when thou doest alms, let not thy left hand know what thy right hand doeth:

That thine alms may be in secret: and thy Father which seeth in secret himself shall reward you openly" (Matthew 6:1-4).

When we pray, when we fast, and when we give, the Bible says that we must be pure in our motives. If we do what we do for the sake of being seen by others, then being seen by others is our only reward. If, however, we do what we do in obedience to God, then God will reward us. If you have ever given tithes and offerings and have not been blessed, this may be the reason for it.

Another reason why God sometimes does not prosper people is that they are involved in sin: laziness, drunkenness, gluttony, or dishonesty. "For the drunkard and the glutton shall come to poverty: and drowsiness shall clothe a man with rags" (Proverbs 23:21); "Yet a little sleep, a little slumber, a little folding of the hands to sleep: So shall thy poverty come as one that traveleth; and thy want as an armed man (Proverbs 24:33, 34). "Bread of deceit is sweet to a man; but afterwards his mouth shall be filled with gravel. . . . an inheritance may be gotten hastily at the beginning: but the end thereof shall not be blessed" (Proverbs 20:17, 21).

Certain sins, according to the Bible, carry with them the penalty of poverty. Just as God gives us more than we give Him in the way of tithes and offerings when we do good, when we do evil God takes from us more than we profited by our sin. People who do evil, the Bible says, "have sown the wind, and they shall reap the whirlwind," (Hosea 8:7).

By far the most common reason, however, that

people sometimes don't prosper when they give their tithes and offerings is the same reason why people don't receive many of God's other blessings: they have not believed that God will do what He says He will do. This is where *what you say* is so important. Saying God will do what He has promised He will do just *does* something in your spirit. Say out loud, "My God shall supply all my need; He said to prove him and I have; I am expecting to receive back many times what I have given." If you continue to *talk* poverty, you will *get* poverty. If you talk prosperity—and you have done your part according to God's principles of giving—then prosperity is what you will get.

Why does God's Word bless some people and not bless others? The Bible says that when people hear God's Word but do not believe it, "the word preached did not profit them, not being mixed with faith in them that heard it" (Hebrews 4:2). Often I too have been guilty of not mixing God's Word with faith.

Before one of my crusade trips to the West Indies, as we approached the departure date, I said to my wife, "Honey, our crusade schedule for the West Indies is less than a month away, and we don't yet have one dollar toward that journey. Jesus said to sit down and count the cost before you try to build a house. Maybe we had better not go now, with such a short time to raise money to pay all our expenses."

My wife, however, has always possessed un-conquerable faith and the belief that God will do incredible things if we have a positive attitude of faith. She answered my negative thinking with,

77

"Now, Don, you know that God has laid this mission field upon our hearts. There's no possible way we can bypass this trip, for we did not call ourselves to this task. This is the Lord's call, and He will provide!"

I began to affirm Philippians 4:19, "But my God shall supply all your need according to his riches in glory by Christ Jesus." From that time on, as I drove my car from place to place, and several times throughout every day, I boldly stated these words, repeating them again and again: "My God shall supply all my needs!" How those words freed my spirit! They strengthened my faith and changed my attitude. Repeating this Scripture to myself, believing, and talking to God worked the miracle I needed.

On two previous missions to the West Indies, we had had to cut short our trip because of lack of enough money to continue. On this trip, however, we fulfilled our entire schedule because God supplied our every need. What was the difference this time? I firmly believe that it was the fact that we clung tenaciously to God's Word, and God, hearing *our* words, felt duly obligated to perform it.

My wife is a constant source of inspiration to me in this matter of God's supplying our needs. Back in 1961, at the same time that I was conducting another crusade, my wife and children were all living in Victoria, British Columbia. Even though the Lord was wonderfully blessing the crusade, the love offering for sustaining my ministry was small and inadequate. This created critical financial problems for all of us; we badly needed more money for paying bills and for maintaining living expenses.

One weekend I went to Victoria to visit my family

briefly before returning to the crusade. Because I had so little money to leave with my wife, I was beginning to feel frustrated. We spent the night talking to God, face to face.

Finally, Joyce prayed, "Dear God, Supplier of all our needs, You know that we have a big problem here. We have very little money. In fact, I don't see how we'll manage *this week*. Perhaps You no longer want Don to continue in this crusade. If You don't, we will understand. We are sure that whatever Your reason would be, it would be a good one. Now, if You do not meet our financial needs, we will give up this ministry to somebody else. We want whatever You want."

Joyce, like Moses of old, had talked right out of her heart to the Lord. And I am totally convinced, as was confirmed very shortly, that our Heavenly Father was well pleased with His child for talking to Him so freely and unashamedly. Her words and God's promise made the difference.

That prayer turned the tide for us, spiritually and financially. Never again were we so poverty-stricken, either in faith or in finances.

One day, while I was standing in the airport in Tortola, I began to talk to a man who turned out to be a salesman. At first, we talked the small talk of two strangers, about why *I* was there, about why *he* was there. As we talked on, we realized that we had much in common: we were both Christians. Finally, he told me that he had a story that he wanted to tell me, a completely unexplainable one by most standards.

"I'm not a strong believer in dreams," he

remarked, "but something happened to me a few years ago that has remained a mystery to me to this day.

"For a number of years," he continued, "I had been traveling for a large wholesale company out of St. Louis, Missouri. On one of my routes, I had one very particular old friend named Brother Benton. The whole town called him that. He nearly always had an order for me. But whether or not he had, I always felt better after making my call on him. He was always so cheerful, and he talked so pleasantly. I could see my customers only twice a year, and I always looked forward to the days I would see *him*.

"On one visit I sold him a much larger order than he had ever given me before, but I did not hesitate to recommend the house to fill the order. I knew that he was universally loved and respected in that town as a sincere Christian. He would not keep alcoholic beverages or tobacco in any form in his store. He had always told me that his Bible condemned both, and he would have nothing to do with them. No amount of talking or any offer of liberal discounts from the tobacco and liquor companies could induce him to deviate from that rule.

"About six months after I had sold him that large order, my head office notified me that his bill was unpaid and that I should call on him as soon as possible and collect it. I hurried over my territory and went in person to look after the matter. When I reached his store, he was not there. Another man was taking his place. I learned that a short time after he had placed that order, he had become ill, and that he and his family had all been sick at different

80

periods for some time. His illness had lasted several months, and he was still confined to his home. I did not see him, but he sent me word that the matter would come out all right in the end.

"He had suffered more losses than he had realized; another six months went by, and the bill was still unpaid. I wrote to my head office and told them the condition of things. At that time, they held up all proceedings against him. Six more months went by, and I was told that I must go at once and either collect the money or enter suit against him. I had no choice in the matter, but I'll tell you, I had some rebellious thoughts.

"The night before I arrived at his town, I could not sleep. I spent several weary hours rolling and tossing on my bed, trying to figure out some way to avoid closing on my old friend. I knew that he was a good man who had his back against the wall through no fault of his own.

"While tossing on my bed, I must have fallen asleep. I dreamed that I was calling on my old friend and that we were sitting in his family room, with all his family around. He turned to me and said, 'We are just about to have our morning devotional service; we will be glad to have you join us.'

"I replied, 'With pleasure.'

"He then said, 'We'll read the Twenty-third Psalm.'

"He began to read, but I was astonished at the words I heard! I had learned that Psalm long ago in Sunday School, and I will never forget that 'The Lord is my Shepherd.'

"My heart rejoiced as I heard the words he read,

although I had never heard them that way before! He read, 'The Lord is my Banker; I shall not fail. He maketh me to lie down in gold mines; He giveth me the combination of His tills. He restoreth my credit; He showeth me how to avoid law suits for His name's sake. Yea, though I walk in the very shadow of debt, I will fear no evil, for Thou art with me; thy silver and thy gold, they rescue me. Thou preparest a way for me in the presence of the collectors; Thou fillest my barrels with oil; my measure runneth over. Surely goodness and mercy shall follow me all the days of my life, and I will do business in the name of the Lord.' Having read the Scripture, he knelt down and prayed. I had never in my life heard such a prayer. He nearly took my breath away when he asked his Heavenly Father to bless me his friend.

"With his 'Amen!' I awoke with a start!

"I had previously planned to call on my friend at his home early in the morning. I got up, dressed, and reached his home just as the sun was coming up.

"He met me at the door with a smile and a hearty handshake. He said, 'Come in, come right in. We are just going to have morning prayers, and we will be glad to have you join us.' He introduced me to his wife and children. He took up his Bible and said, 'We'll read the Twenty-third Psalm.' He read it in a clear, strong voice, but he read it just as it is written in the Bible. I cannot tell you my feelings and thoughts as he read. We knelt in prayer, and he humbly made known to God his wishes; but his prayer did not sound like the one I had heard in my dream, though he appeared to have covered the same thoughts. He told the Lord he owed some money, and that it was past due; he asked that a way might open so that he could pay it that very day. He then prayed for me. While I was on my knees there, I resolved that for one time in my life, I was going to disobey orders!

"After prayers, we both went directly to his store. Just as we entered the store, a young man met us, saying, 'Brother Benton, Father sent me over to tell you that he would take the house and lot that he is interested in buying from you, the one that he talked about the other day. He told me to give you this money and to tell you that he will pay the balance when you settle.'

"The old man took the money. Tears began to roll down his cheeks as he turned away. He wrote the young man a receipt for the money and gave it to him. He then turned to his ledger and began to figure. He turned to me and said, 'Will you kindly receipt this bill?' I saw that he had added interest for all the months that he had not been able to pay. When I told him that I had been instructed to forgo the interest, he declined the offer. He said that he wanted to pay all his just debts and that he was grateful for the extra time the company had given him. I took the money and sent it in to my office in St. Louis.

"At the same time that I had been tossing on my bed that morning, my old friend was on his knees in his room, pleading with his Banker for a loan. I was very much gratified when he got it, and ever since that day, when I become discouraged, I apply the Twenty-third Psalm as the remedy."

When things are going well, it is easy to call the

Lord your Shepherd and vow to follow Him all the days of your life. To all of us, though, comes the times of walking in the valley. *Then* God takes our measure. He still wants to hear us say, "My God will supply all my needs," and mean it. Brother Benton's faith was fixed firmly on God, and his words proved it. God honored him by fulfilling his need.

GOD GIVETH WEALTH AND HEALTH

This "power poem" is one some will not easily trust. It has been looked upon to be "unspiritual" to have wealth. And even the gift of health from God is generally pictured as not likely to be obtained.

The word "wealth" means resources, competence to meet our obligations. God doesn't promise to make us millionaires. But He does provide for our every need (Philippians 4:19) and assures our prosperity and good success if we live by His Word (Joshua 1:8). Delight in the Word of God, meditate in it and God says that whatsoever you do will prosper (Psalm 1:1-3).

Jesus said, "Seek ye first the kingdom of God and His righteousness, and all these things shall be added unto you" (Matthew 6:33). Jesus was here speaking about our material provisions (food, raiment, shelter). Jesus did **not** say that if we seek first the kingdom of God, all these things will be **taken away** from you. No, He said all these things—our material provisions—**shall be added unto us!**

The Bible says, "It is God who giveth thee the power to get wealth" (Deuteronomy 8:18). And it is Satan's business to impoverish our lives, to ruin our Christian effectiveness in paying our obligations. Satan seeks to bring us to embarrassment in financial matters. Agree with God; disagree with the devil!

God says, "Beloved, I wish above all things that thou mayest prosper and be in health, even as thy soul prospereth" (3 John 2). This is God's "big wish" for us, His children, that we may prosper and be in health, **even as our souls prosper!** How do we prosper in our souls? (1) By Spirit-led prayer, and a positive praise life; (2) By studying God's Word and confessing the Scriptures boldly; (3) By witnessing with our lives and lips of Christ to others.

When so many of God's people are afflicted and poverty-stricken, and the work of God is reduced to a standstill in some quarters because of lack of finances, it's high time we affirmed these scriptures quoted here, to receive the benefit of God's gifts of wealth and health.

Daily speak it boldly: GOD GIVETH ME WEALTH AND HEALTH!

Chapter Nine

HOW TO CAST OUT EVIL SPIRITS

"It was three o'clock in the morning," Earl Britain said. "I turned over in bed and put out my hand to touch my wife. She wasn't there!" With those words, my friend began his account of how he learned his power against the devil.

"I thought she must have gotten up for some reason," he continued. "I was worried about her—she'd been acting strangely for weeks. Quickly I looked through the other bedrooms and the bathroom. Then I ran to the basement to see if she'd gone down there for some reason. But she was nowhere in the house!

"My heart sank. She had been sick, and in the past few months she had seemed to be suffering mentally. She had literally been withdrawing from life. Though I had prayed much, she had grown worse steadily. Nothing I said or did seemed to have any effect on her.

"I ran into the bedroom and quickly pulled on my clothes and shoes. I grabbed a coat and started for the front door. All during that time, I kept pleading, 'God, please let her be all right; please don't let her get hurt!'

"When I opened the door to go out, she was standing there, wet, wild-eyed, and with her hair streaming over her face. She had been out in the rain in only her nightgown and her slippers, which were now mud-soaked.

"As I reached out for her and drew her to me, trying to keep my anxiety out of my voice, I questioned her, 'Where have you been? I have been so worried!'

"'I just went for a walk in the woods; I didn't feel sleepy, and I thought that it might be good for me,' she explained.

"She had never before done anything so dangerous as this. From the unnatural expression in her eyes and from her complete lack of awareness of the seriousness of what she had done, I was afraid that she was near the breaking point; she seemed close to some kind of collapse.

"I put my arm around her and took her back into the bedroom. I stayed with her until she had put on dry clothing and was back in bed. When I felt that she had gone to sleep, I got up. I couldn't sleep. I couldn't even sit still. Countless questions ran through my mind: 'What will happen to her next? What will she do? Is there no answer?'

"Something had to be done, but *what*? I had been asking God to help her: 'Heal her, dear God, please heal her. Do it, Lord; do it, in Jesus' name.' I had prayed over and over for her recovery.

"Suddenly I recalled the scripture, 'Behold, I give you power over all the power of the enemy' (Luke 10:19). Perhaps God was telling me to use another approach to this problem. Perhaps I had not exhausted my own power before asking for His. I began to pray for guidance.

"As I walked the floor in those early morning hours, seeking for some word from God, some weapon to use against the devil, whose crafty treachery I was now sure was working in my wife, these words of Jesus struck my mind: 'The prince of this world cometh, but he hath no part in me' (John 14:30). As a drowning man grabs a lifebelt thrown to him, I grasped those words.

"My mood changed. This time my words were not words of pleading. Neither were they words of praise. These words spoke to the devil. Over and over I declared to Satan, 'You have no power over her. You have no part of her. She does not belong to herself. She belongs to Jesus Christ, Who paid a price for her. You are an intruder here.'

"As I paced the floor, I continued to repeat this aloud. Then I became bolder. Possibly what had opened the door to Satan in our home concerned *me* and not my wife! Perhaps it was *my* soul he was seeking! He knew my deep love and concern for her, and it almost seemed he was trying to barter with me, using her as the price.

"I became bolder and bolder then. 'Neither have you any part of *me*. We both belong to Jesus. Our lives and all our possessions are dedicated to Him. You have no power over either of us. You have no power over anything in this home. You have no business here.'

"Physically, mentally, and spiritually I battled for an hour, telling the devil that my wife and I were blood-bought possessions of Jesus Christ. I felt Satan's evil presence right there in that room. I knew I was face to face with him. But I realized, also, that I had the power of Jesus to command the enemy to leave. I had power over all the power of the enemy and Jesus had told me that 'nothing shall by any means hurt you' (Luke 10:19).

"Finally, as Jesus' assurance of victory seeped through my mind and body, I walked to the door, opened it, and turned to the devil, just as if he had been embodied there. I commanded, 'In the name of Jesus, get out!'

"And he did! Immediately, I felt his presence lifted from that room. It was a definite sensation. Just as, earlier, I had detected his presence in my spirit, now I knew by the spirit quite definitely that he was gone. Light seemed to fill the room, which shortly before had been oppressively dark.

"I walked into the bedroom and over to my wife's bed. She had awakened from my loud talking; but on her face was a smile, and a light shone in her eyes. I had not seen a light like that in her eyes for a long time! Today she is just as healthy mentally as she instantly became that morning when Jesus Christ demonstrated to us His victory over the devil."

As my friend Earl Britain learned, the forces of

evil are growing, and strangely perilous events are happening in every area of the world. In these last days, it is important to keep in mind God's promise that "When the enemy shall come in like a flood, the Spirit of the Lord shall lift up a standard against him" (Isaiah 59:19). We must courageously face the fact that Satan is doing his strongest and vilest work in these last days—but we must also remember that God's Spirit is stronger than the enemy.

As Christians, we do not need to worry about Satan, or be frustrated by his tactics. Instead, it is our right and duty to challenge the devil boldly in Jesus' name. "In my name," Jesus promised, "they shall cast out devils" (Mark 16:17). We have the power of Jesus' name at our command.

Satan sometimes tries to fool us into thinking that sin is enjoyable. Unfortunately, it is only enjoyable to begin with—before we realize that we have been made its servant. Actually, demons are behind the godless activities and the destructive elements we see in the world today. Demons fire men's brains and senses with lust for drink, drugs, and deliquency; they cause people to lose control and commit shameful acts of immorality; demons break up homes and ruin marriages; demons are behind the enormous growth of sorrow, bitterness, pain, violence, and confusion going on around us.

Even scientists, psychiatrists and medical men recognize that some strange supernatural power has been unleashed in this critical hour. We Christians especially must not be ignorant of Satan's devices, which he uses to twist and tangle people's minds, to saturate lives with filth and rot, and to drag human souls into a Christless eternity "where there is weeping and wailing and gnashing of teeth."

We need to recognize our enemy for the ugly, hateful spirit he is—the cause of the world's sorrow and heartache. Then we can deal boldly against the devil and his demons with the weapons of our warfare: the Word of God, the name of Jesus, the blood of Christ. The devil is our adversary—he's the thief who comes to steal, kill, destroy. The Bible says the devil is our enemy. We must treat him as such.

Little though it's taught, a large part of the ministry of Jesus—about one-fourth—was spent in casting out devils. One would sometimes think, in listening to the average sermon, that demons had gone out of existence, or that they had been herded together in the slums of the city or were spending their time deluding the members of some other denomination.

I cannot conceive how successful work can be done today, or how believers can be in a place of continual victory, unless they know that the source of their danger lies in demonic power, and that the power to conquer it is in the name of Jesus of Nazareth, the Son of God.

The more quickly we recognize that the very air about us is filled with hostile forces who are attempting to destroy our fellowship with the Father and to deprive us of our usefulness is His service, the better it will be for us. To ignore the existence of demons only gives the adversary a greater advantage over us.

In my travels as an evangelist, I have found that

people are hungry for the Lord; they want deliverance; they crave eternal life; but they are unable, many of them, to break loose from the bonds that are holding them in sin.

Hundreds of people have indicated their sincere desire to be saved. They have said, "I cannot become a Christian. I want to, but something holds me." I met a young man like this in Lodi, California. He wanted salvation, but an unseen power held him back. I simply laid my hand on his shoulder and said, "In the name of Jesus Christ, I command the power that holds you broken. Now in His mighty name, let's pray." With tears of joy, he obeyed.

After that man was saved, I stood amazed at the effect. A feeling of awe came over me that I had been able to exercise, by a simple command in Jesus' name, this marvelous power, and since that time, I have seen many startling results in revival services through using His name.

"In my name ye shall cast out demons." In the name of Jesus we have broken demons' power over meetings, homes, and sometimes entire communities.

As Christians, our combat is not against flesh and blood, but against the principalities and powers in heavenly places; our war is against demons of all ranks, kinds, and authorities. They are attacking mankind everywhere, and they are especially challenging the children of God.

I have prayed with men who were held by habits—tobacco, liquor, lusts—and in the mighty name of Jesus I have seen them delivered, usually instantaneously.

I have found many Christians who were unable to testify with freedom in public meetings, who felt their mouths closed while their hearts cried for liberty. I have used Jesus' name and commanded the demon power broken, and testimonies have been restored, power in prayer given. What joy is brought to lives through the delivering name of Jesus Christ!

Three things are necessary in order to take deliverance and victory over demons:

First, we must be the children of God.

Second, we must not have any unconfessed or unforgiven sin in our hearts, for if we do, the demons will laugh at our prayers.

Third, we must know the power of the name of Jesus, and know how to use it. Read the book of Acts carefully and notice how the disciples used His name.

If your own life has been defeated and hemmed in by the power of the adversary, rise up in that almighty name of Jesus: hurl back the enemy; take your deliverance; go and set others free!

I had never prayed for the sick or cast out devils in my ministry to any degree until I received the revelation of the authority of the name of Jesus.

When we learn to use the name of Jesus according to the Word, in the power of the Spirit, we have the secret which shook the world through the apostles.

In 2 Thessalonians 1:12, Paul prays "that the name of our Lord Jesus Christ may be glorified in you and ye in him." How could His name be glorified more in us than to use it as the early Church did?

HOW TO CAST OUT
EVIL SPIRITS

1. Know your enemy. "Not ignorant of Satan's devices" (2 Corinthians 2:11), learn by the Spirit to discern the presence and work of evil spirits (1 Corinthians 12:10).

2. Know your rights. You are an *overcomer* of all of Satan's work because of the blood of Jesus, and the word of your testimony (Revelation 12:11). Christ has given you power and authority over all the power of the devil (Luke 10:19). Dare to use it.

3. Your ground for sure victory is that Jesus defeated Satan, stripped him of his authority, and rose the eternal Victor! With "Christ in you" count heavily on this unshakable fact: "Greater is he that is within you than he that is in the world" (1 John 4:4). Daily make this your personal testimony!

4. Boldly quote the Words of God against Satan, as Jesus did (Matthew 4). The Word is weapon Number One (2 Corinthians 10:4); when the enemy comes in like a flood the Spirit of the Lord lifts up a standard—the Word—against him (Isaiah 59:19). Quote the Word aloud often to rout the enemy!

5. There are captives all around you that "ought to be loosed" from every bond of Satan (Luke 13:16). In the mighty name of Jesus, you

can be God's instrument to liberate people from every kind of evil spirit.

6. Jesus said, "In my name shall ye cast out devils [demons, evil spririts]" (Mark 16:17). Say, "In the name of Jesus, I command you evil spirits to depart." Stand your ground fearlessly, without wavering! Evil spirits know they must submit to the name of Jesus! Read Philippians 2:9-11.

7. Refuse to be Satan's "dumping ground" where evil spirits produce mental unsoundness, nervous disorders, spirits of gloom, heaviness and depression, physical infirmities and diseases, spiritual bondages. "Resist the devil and he will flee from you" (James 4:7).

8. Plead the power of the blood of Jesus. Live under the blood by walking in the light. "If we walk in the light, as he is in the light, we have fellowship one with another, and the blood of Jesus Christ cleanseth us from all sin" (1 John 1:7). Boldly speak God's Word against Satan. We are in a real warfare (Ephesians 6:12-16). Casting out evil spirits is acting in the unseen "spirit-realm" where you rely on the anointing of the Spirit as Jesus did. Read Luke 4:18-19 and Acts 10:38. Put on the whole armor of God. Wax bold against evil spirits in the name of Jesus. You are "more than a conqueror through Christ" (Romans 8:37). Victory is certain through Jesus!

Chapter Ten

WHAT'S IN A NAME?

"In the name of Jesus I curse you, spirit of infirmity, and command you to leave this body."

Those were the unforgettable words of William W. Freeman, as he ministered to my mother in May, 1948. My mother left the platform with a spring in her step; I was so excited I left my seat to meet her halfway down the aisle.

"How are you, Mom?" I eagerly inquired.

"I am just perfect," my mother replied with tears streaming down her face. "I just felt a hot sensation go through my whole back; I know the Lord has healed me!"

That miracle my mother received was indeed electrifying. It stirred the faith of the people in the meeting. And to me, personally, it was God's way of answering a prayer for the salvation of my family. When they witnessed the transformation she received in her body, my family gladly accepted

Jesus as personal Savior. This was not the first miracle in Jesus' name I had witnessed. Shortly before this night, I had gone as a young Baptist minister with friends to Dr. Thomas Wyatt's Wings of Healing Temple in Portland, Oregon, where Evangelist Freeman was ministering. There I had for the first time encountered the power of the name of Jesus. When Brother Freeman had commanded diseases and afflictions to leave people's bodies, I saw the evidence of the enormous power that lies in Jesus' name.

In Acts 3:16 Peter explains the healing of the lame man at the Gate Beautiful. "And his name, through faith in his name, hath made this man strong, whom ye see and know: yea, the faith which is by him hath given him this perfect soundness in the presence of you all."

The name of Jesus had wrought a miracle for the lame man, and it is faith in this name that brings supernatural results when we use this name today.

A year later, in 1949, Brother Freeman invited me to travel with him in his gigantic crusades that were stirring cities for Christ. Brother Freeman was fearless in using the name of Jesus in ministering to all kinds of cases. The average service was on this order:

He preached the Gospel with rich anointing. It was strictly a salvation message to win the unsaved. He always emphasized the importance of salvation of the soul, even before the healing of the body. "First things first," he would insist as he was used of the Holy Spirit to influence hundreds to receive the Savior by faith.

Then he would ask for those to come forward who were totally deaf in one or both ears, blind in one or both eyes, without a sense of smell or taste; also those who suffered with cancer, tuberculosis, goiters, tumors and ruptures.

Usually about two hundred people would respond to this invitation. Then Brother Freeman and I would walk among these people. By the gift of the Spirit, he could perceive who was "ready" to receive his or her miracle. Then he would send these people to the platform. (Later, I learned to exercise this same gift of the Spirit to "know" who was ready, and who needed to wait for a time.)

On the platform, Brother Freeman would begin— usually with someone who was totally deaf in one ear.

Literally hundreds of times I heard and watched him speak these words: "In the name of Jesus, I take authority and dominion over you spirits of deafness. In the name of Jesus, I command you deaf spirits to come out of this ear. Now I command you to receive your hearing and be made whole!"

The results were indisputable. Person after person, when tested, demonstrated that whereas they had been deaf in that ear, they could now hear perfectly. "And his name, through faith in his name, hath made this man whole!"

Then it was the same in ministering to other kinds of afflictions: sight came into blind eyes and ruptures, tumors, and goiters disappeared through the power of the name of Jesus spoken by God's servant.

I witnessed healings and miracles of all descriptions in the months I travelled with Brother Freeman in 1949. Then Joyce and I were married in 1950. After our honeymoon, we went with Brother Freeman to Los Angeles where he used the same big tent Billy Graham had used the year before for his historic crusade. Demos Shakarian, later President of the Full Gospel Businessmen International, was chairman of the William Freeman Los Angeles Crusade.

There were 7,000 chairs under the tent. Nightly for five solid weeks these chairs were filled, often with thousands standing on the outside.

Again I saw the power of the name of Jesus in operation, as tremendous miracles were wrought.

I was thoroughly convinced there was power in the name of Jesus to produce astounding miracles. But I always thought to myself that the use of that name in such effectiveness was limited to a man like Brother Freeman, because he had seen an angel and heard the voice of God direct him to the healing ministry. I appreciated the name of Jesus. I admired the authority vested in that name. I prayed to the Father in the name. But I didn't have the same confidence or faith in the name of Jesus that Brother Freeman had.

In April, 1951, I was invited to conduct a crusade at a church. I was hungering for a visitation of God's power, but it seemed as though this was being denied me. One morning I arose early and told my wife I was going to the church to "pray until God visits me."

I was on my knees for two hours of earnest prayer. While I was broken before God by His Spirit, I arose from my knees and took a seat on the altar where I had been kneeling. Frankly, I felt keen disappointment that God had not "visited me" as I was craving.

Then I opened my Bible to Philippians chapter two and began to read. When I read verses 9 to 11, my heart was illuminated by this passage:

"Wherefore God also hath highly exalted him, and given him a name which is above every name: That at the name of Jesus every knee should bow, of things in heaven, and things in earth, and things under the earth; And that every tongue should confess that Jesus Christ is Lord, to the glory of God the Father."

As I read and re-read this passage, the Holy Spirit was pouring a staggering revelation into my understanding. God the Father had so exalted His Son Jesus, that He had given Him the name above every name in heaven, earth and hell! "All things" in heaven, earth, and hell must bow to the name of Jesus!

I began to think of great names of history; great names of our present day; great names that represented wealth, position, fame. But God had decreed the name of Jesus was supreme above all these names! Hallelujah! I could hardly comprehend what had been revealed to me. While "the visitation of God" had not come to me that morning by the appearance of an angel, or the audible voice of God, indeed He had visited me by His divine Word through the revelation of the Holy Spirit. I would never be the same again! "If the name of Jesus is superior to all names or things," I reasoned, "then I can subdue diseases, demons, difficulties in the power of this name!"

I could hardly wait for the next opportunity to exercise this new faith I had . . . that I could speak the name of Jesus with full faith just as I had seen Brother Freeman do thousands of times.

It was only a short time until I was to have the opportunity to speak the name of Jesus against a terrifying destroyer. I received a phone call from a lady we called Grandma Davis.

"Brother Gossett, I am calling you because I know you have traveled with Brother Freeman," she stated. "My grandson has been given up to die with brain tumors, and his parents are bringing him to my home Sunday afternoon."

Grandma Davis went on to explain, "Now I just felt with your having seen hundreds of people healed when Brother Freeman prays, that I should call you to come and pray for my grandson." Brain tumors! Given up to die! Those "things" fit into the category of what God had given us power over in the name of Jesus. I could hardly wait to speak that name against the brain tumors.

When Joyce and I were ushered into the Davis home that Sunday afternoon, we found a decided "funeral atmosphere." The nine-year-old grandson had been given up to die; family members had gathered to see the boy alive for possibly the last time; death was expected at any time.

This grim environment failed to dim my confidence in the name of Jesus on my lips. Readily I placed my hands upon the boy, and spoke with full authority. "In the name of Jesus, I rebuke these brain tumors. You foul spirits of affliction, I command you in the name of Jesus to loose your death-hold upon this boy, and go in Jesus' name."

Praise the Lord! While there were no visible evidences of any miracle, inside I was convinced a miracle was being wrought. I left that home knowing that I had been engaged in a life-and-death conflict, but I was at peace in my heart. I knew the power of the name of Jesus to dispel even deadly brain tumors.

Shortly afterwards the parents took the boy back to the hospital where new tests were made on the boy. To the amazement of the specialists, they could find no trace of brain tumors. The name of Jesus had triumphed!

"And his name, through faith in his name, hath made this man whole."

Many years later, I met this boy's uncle. He came to my crusade and shared a public testimony of this miracle. He told us that the boy was now married and had a family. He was supposed to have died at age nine!

I rejoined Brother Freeman for his crusades under the big tent at Fresno and Modesto where scores of churches united for evangelism. Twice daily I was busy conducting radio broadcasts in connection with the crusades on radio stations in Lodi and Modesto.

Driving down the highway, I would bask in the

blessing of the name of Jesus. I would sing for hours in praising the name of Jesus in songs and choruses.

> Jesus, O how sweet the Name!
> Jesus, every day the same!
> Jesus, let all earth proclaim,
> His worthy praise forever!

One morning I had just concluded my broadcast on KCVR, the Lodi station. As I turned on to the highway, I saw a young man hitch-hiking. I felt a tug in my heart that I should offer him a ride.

"How far are you going?" I asked him.

"About ten miles down the road," he answered.

I knew I would be there in about fifteen minutes, so I started sharing Jesus with him.

Immediately he responded, "Man, I'm glad you are talking to me about religion. I've always wanted to become a Christian."

I was delighted. Usually I meet with opposition or indifference when I share Jesus with others. He went on to explain, "I went to a Baptist Sunday School as a boy. I heard about getting saved then. I always wanted to be saved, but somehow I just can't be saved."

He sincerely felt that he was predestined to be lost forever. Somewhere, he had heard the false teaching that one individual is predestined to be saved, but the next individual is predestined to be lost.

I tried carefully to share with him the Bible facts that "whosoever will" may be saved. But my words were unconvincing. He had been deceived to believe that he was doomed to be eternally separated from

God because it was predestined that way long before he was born.

Finally, we reached his destination. I pulled my car to the curb and shared with him:

"It's not by chance or accident that I picked you up this morning. The Lord loves you, and He wants to save you. I've shared with you several Bible verses that prove that. Right now, by faith open your life to Christ here in my car."

The man grasped the door handle. "No thanks, I would love to be saved, but I just can't be. Thanks, anyway," he sadly shook his head.

Suddenly the Holy Spirit showed me the situation:

Here was a man who wanted Jesus. The Lord doesn't save anyone against his will. Each individual is a free moral agent to accept or reject Jesus Christ. This man craved Eternal Life.

I was startled when the Spirit revealed to me the vile work of the devil, who blinds minds and eyes to the truth. Before he opened the door to get out, I heard myself speaking these Spirit-anointed words: "Devil, in the name of Jesus, take your hands off this man. He desires salvation from Jesus Christ, and you have deceived him long enough."

I hardly spoke this command until the man turned toward me, tears in his eyes. "I am ready to pray," he spoke anxiously.

And pray we did. I led him to Jesus Christ as personal Savior and Lord of his life. He was overjoyed. The presence of God was very near that roadside prayer meeting!

After counselling with the young man further,

giving him Bible instructions on what had happened in his life, I bade him farewell.

As I drove away in my car I was mystified to realize the authority I had exercised in Jesus' name—authority that could release a young man from satanic control in an instant.

Later, I tried taking this authority with whole groups. For instance, I would observe a whole row of people who were under the conviction of the Holy Spirit, but were not responding to the invitation. I would leave the platform, walk to the back of the church and invite them to come to Christ.

Then I would speak these words: "In the name of Jesus, I command Satan's power to be broken over each of your lives. Now in Jesus' mighty name, come and receive the Savior!" Praise the Lord, almost one hundred percent of them would respond every time.

I have done the same thing over large audiences of the unsaved. As I speak the name of Jesus, commanding satanic dominion to be broken, the unsaved respond to receive the new birth.

I have witnessed thousands of healing miracles after the name of Jesus has been spoken. First, there were the five years I was in those tremendous crusades with William W. Freeman. Later, I saw similar miracles when I did some writing for evangelist Jack Coe. In 1959-60 I was editor of *Faith Digest*, T.L. Osborn's magazine. I witnessed the same authority exercised in his ministry; it resulted in nations' being stirred.

In my own ministry, I have ministered healing to hundreds who were totally deaf in one or both ears,

106

by speaking the name of Jesus. I have seen hundreds of arthritis victims delivered in this name.

In overseas crusades where the masses assemble to hear the Gospel, I have usually ministered a mass prayer for all the sick. After I boldly speak the name of Jesus, scores of people bear witness to instant and wonderful healings received.

We do not use the name of Jesus as a fetish or a charm. We speak His name with intelligence, based upon clear instructions given in the Word of God.

THE NAME OF JESUS

1. Because "God hath highly exalted him, and given him the name which is above every name" in heaven, earth and hell (Philippians 2:9-11), I boldly speak His name in subduing all other names.

2. Because "Whatsoever I ask in His name, that will He do, that the Father might be glorified in the son" (John 14:13), I confidently speak in His name, that the Father might be glorified.

3. Because "If I ask any thing in His name, He will do it" (John 14:14), I know that **any thing** includes salvation, healing, supply of needs, liberation.

4. Because "Whatsoever I ask the Father in Jesus' name, He will give it to me" (John 16:23), I pray always to my Father in the name of His beloved Son.

5. Because He said, "Hitherto ye have asked nothing in My name; ask that your joy might be full" (John 16:24), my joy is overflowing because of great and mighty answers.

6. With Peter I fearlessly declare, "Such as I have give I thee, in the name of Jesus rise up" (Acts 3:6).

7. Because "His name, through faith in His name, makes strong and perfect soundness," (Acts 3:16), I confess childlike faith in Jesus' name.

8. "Whatsoever I do in word or deed, I do all in the name of the Lord Jesus, giving thanks to God and the Father by him" (Colossians 3:17).

9. "In the name of Jesus I cast out demons" (Mark 16:17); therefore I possess total authority over the works of Satan.

10. "I give thanks always for all things unto God in the name of the Lord Jesus Christ" (Ephesians 5:20).

11. I do not use the name of Jesus as a fetish or charm; I know His name represents "all power in heaven and in earth" (Matthew 28:18).

12. "All hail the power of Jesus' name" is more than an anthem; I hail the power of His saving, healing, delivering name... the matchless name of Jesus.

Chapter Eleven

YOU CAN DO THAT

When I was editor of *Faith Digest* at Tulsa, Oklahoma, my esteemed friend evangelist T.L. Osborn shared with me the following account:

"I was visiting a service in the Civic Auditorium in Portland, Oregon. I was sitting in the third balcony.

"Following the message, a long line of people passed before the minister for his prayers for healing. He stopped a deaf and dumb child and, placing his fingers to her ears, said: 'Thou deaf and dumb spirit, I adjure thee in the name of Jesus Christ, leave the child and enter her no more.' He spoke calmly, but with absolute certainty. The child was perfectly healed. How those words rang in my soul! *'I adjure thee in the name of Jesus Christ!'*

"I had never heard a man pray like that. He had no question. He spoke softly, yet with irresistible force. There was indisputable authority in his voice. He invoked the name of Jesus and a demon was compelled to obey.

"I saw the name of Jesus demonstrated. It changed my life.

"Jesus was alive. He was on the platform. I could not see Him, but when that pastor invoked His name, He was there. *He* backed up that command. I saw Jesus in His name that night.

"A thousand voices whirled over my head as I sat there weeping. They said: *'You can do that! You can do that! That is what Peter and Paul did! That proves the Bible is good today! You can do that!'*

"'Yes!' I said. 'I can do that! Jesus is alive! He is here! He is with me! I can use His name! I can cast out devils! Yes, I can do that!'

"I walked out of that auditorium a new man. Jesus and I were walking together. I would use His name and compel devils to come out and diseases to die. I could speak in His name. Jesus would do the miracle. No demon or disease would resist *His authority. They would be under His ultimatum when I would use HIS name.*

"For years now I have proclaimed His name in over thirty countries. Around the world I have beheld the glory of Jesus Christ by exalting His name among the heathen. In every campaign we have conducted overseas, the Lord Jesus Christ has appeared at least once, and often repeatedly."

"Wherefore God also hath highly exalted him, and given him a name which is above every name: that at the name of Jesus every knee should bow, of things in heaven [angels], and things in earth [men], and things under the earth [demons]" (Philippians 2:9-11).

Do you know what a power of attorney is? It is a written document which authorizes one person to act for another. If someone has given you an unlimited power of attorney, you may sign his checks, you may sell his business, you may do anything you wish on his behalf—and you may do it *in His name*!

Jesus has given us His power of attorney. We have a written document—the Bible—in which Jesus says, "Whatsoever ye shall ask the Father in my name, he will give it you" (John 16:23). Even on a purely legal basis, once we become Christians, we have the right to use Jesus' name. We have the right to "sign" Jesus' name to the "checks" we draw on the "bank" of heaven!

When we accept Jesus as our Savior, we are given Jesus' name to use. Jesus tells us, "Hitherto have ye asked nothing in my name: ask, and ye shall receive, that your joy may be full" (John 16:24). "And whatsoever ye shall ask in my name, that will I do, that the Father may be glorified in the Son" (John 14:13).

Demons, diseases, and circumstances are all subject to this name. This name of Jesus is the majestic name above every name. The Father has willed it. The Holy Ghost bears witness to it. And countless miracles give testimony to the dominion of this name.

Some years ago, a group of hymnbook publishers selected the hymn, "All Hail the Power of Jesus' Name," as the *grand anthem* of the church.

We can all hail the power of Jesus' name, for it is through His name that we have (1) *Salvation* for our souls, (2) *Healing* for our bodies, (3) *Victory* over the

112

forces of Satan, and (4) *Access* to the Father in prayer.

The name of Jesus is inseparably connected with salvation. The very name is filled with music to a repentant soul. "And she shall bring forth a son, and thou shalt call His name JESUS: for He shall save His people from their sins" (Matthew 1:21). "Neither is there salvation in any other: for there is none other name under heaven given among men, whereby we must be saved" (Acts 4:12).

The name of Jesus is the one name through which the sinner can approach the great Father God; it is the one name that gives him a hearing; it is the one name that unveils the mediatorial ministry of Jesus.

Multitudes have received the new birth by simply calling on this name, for *"Whosoever shall call upon the name of the Lord shall be saved"* (Romans 10:13).

Have *you* called on His name? Have you pronounced the name of JESUS in prayer? If not, do it now. His peace will flood your soul. As you call upon His name, see Him lifted up, bleeding, dying, that *you* might live. Your sins will melt away as His life pours into your very being. Call upon His name now and be saved. *You can do that!*

The name of Jesus is the healing name. In Acts 3, the power vested in the name of Jesus is demonstrated mightily. To a helpless cripple sitting in the dirt, Peter said, "In the name of Jesus Christ of Nazareth rise up and walk." Suddenly those useless ankles and feet received strength and that man rushed into the temple, leaping, jumping and shouting praises to God.

The multitude recognized him as a former cripple

and gathered around in wonder and amazement. Peter then told the crowd that the living miracle-working Christ had performed this healing. He climaxed his message with this statement: "And his name [the name of Jesus], through faith in his name, hath made this man strong, whom ye see and know: yea, the faith which is by him hath given him this perfect soundness in the presence of you all" (Acts 3:16).

Thousands of times I have seen the power of the Living Christ manifested in miracles as I have commanded diseases to die and demons to come out in the name of Jesus Christ.

Oh, the bliss of seeing withered limbs stricken by polio suddenly become strong and new—of seeing bodies eaten by cancer suddenly restored! I tell you, there is healing in the name of Jesus. And faith in His wonderful name will make *you* whole right now.

Call upon His name now. Charge your disease to go now, in His name. It cannot stand. You too will be made whole. Receive your healing in His name now. *You can do that!*

The name of Jesus is the commanding name. The Gospels repeatedly tell us about the way in which Jesus combated evil forces: "He preached . . . throughout all Galilee, and cast out devils" (Mark 1:39). There are countless references to Jesus' ministry of casting out demons. It became such an issue that His opposers mistakenly claimed that "He casteth out devils through the prince of devils" (Matthew 9:34).

One would almost think by reading our modern religious literature, and by listening to the average preacher's sermon, that demons had gone out of existence. There are thousands of preachers and Christians who have never in their lives cast out a devil in Jesus' name.

I've never been able to understand how believers can expect to live a life of victory, unless they recognize that their enemy is a demonic power, and that the *power to conquer* is in the name of Jesus, the Son of God.

To ignore the fact of demons only gives the adversary a greater advantage.

Our combat is not against flesh and blood but against the principalities and powers in heavenly places; our war is against demons of all ranks and authorities (Ephesians 6:12). "In my name shall ye cast out devils" was Jesus' promise to "them that believe" (Mark 16:17).

Every disciple whom Jesus sent forth to preach was *commanded* to "cast out devils" (Matthew 10:8). But this promise in Mark 16:17 is not only for "preachers;" it is for every "believer." That includes you—"unto the end of the world."

When you know that you heart is right with God, rise up in the name of Jesus and cast out devils. Drive the enemy out. Act on Christ's promise. Speak with authority. You have the right to use that name. Do not be intimidated. Be courageous. *You* are a "believer." Take your place. Possess victory over the forces of Satan by using this name.

The name of Jesus is the commanding name! Jesus declared, "Whatsoever ye shall ask [or command] in My name, that will I do, that the Father may be glorified in the Son."

Command your disease to go. Command your

enemy to retreat. Take your deliverance. Then go and set others free. Do it now! *You can do that.*

What a marvel that every person born into the family of God is born into Royalty—Divine Royalty. He "hath translated us into the Kingdom of His dear Son" (Colossians 1:13). "Ye are a chosen generation, a *royal* priesthood" (1 Peter 2:9).

Being "born again" into the imperial family, you inherit the right to use the imperial name. What an inheritance! It is always the Father's delight to recognize any petition made in the imperial name. When you pray, you are a member of the imperial family making a request based on your family right—the right to use Jesus' name.

When Jesus says, "Whatsoever ye shall ask the Father in my name, he will give it you," He is giving you a signed check on the entire resources of heaven, and asking you to fill it in. *What a privilege!*

It would pay any Christian to make an exhaustive study of the book of Acts and of the Epistles, to see how this name of Jesus touched every phase of the early Church.

When *you* learn to use the name of Jesus according to the Word, in the power of the Spirit, you have *the secret which shook the world* through the Apostles. Begin to use the name of Jesus in your prayer life today.

"Hitherto have ye asked nothing in my name: ask, and ye shall receive, that your joy may be full" (John 16:24).

Fullness of joy awaits you as you ask the Father boldly in the name of Jesus! You will find something in the name of Jesus that will give joy in a measure you have never before known.

"These signs shall follow them that believe." That means YOU. "In my name shall they cast out devils..."

Take your place. Use the name. It belongs to you. It is the family name. *You* belong to Jesus. *You* are born into His family. *You* are translated into His Kingdom. Delight the Father by being bold and by possessing your rights. Claim your own inheritance, then set other captives free. *You can do that*.

"And whatsoever ye do in word or deed, do all in the name of the Lord Jesus, giving thanks to God and the Father by Him." (Colossians 3:17).

WHAT YOU CAN DO

1. "I can do all things through Christ which strengthens me" (Philippians 4:13). The Bible is God's Word. When God says a thing, He means it. I can do what God says I can do!

2. Jesus said, "In my name shall they cast out devils... They shall lay hands on the sick and they shall recover" (Mark 16:17-18). I can do that! In his name I can cast out demons, and minister healing to the sick.

3. Psalm 37:4 says, "Delight thyself also in the Lord, and he shall give thee the desires of thine heart." I can have the desires of my heart, for I am delighting myself in the Lord!

4. Acts 1:8 says, "Ye shall receive power after that the Holy Ghost is come upon you, and ye shall be witnesses unto me." I can witness in power for I have the Holy Spirit in my life!

5. Isaiah 53:5 proclaims that "With His stripes we are healed." I can possess healing and health for by His stripes I am healed!

6. "Love one another, as I have loved you" (John 13:34). I can love others even as Jesus loved me, for His love is shed abroad in my heart. I love with His love!

7. 1 Corinthians 1:30 says, "Christ Jesus is made unto us wisdom from God." I can have divine wisdom in every crisis, for Christ Himself is my very wisdom.

8. "The righteous are bold as a lion" (Proverbs 28:1). I can be bold as a lion, for I have been made righteous with His righteousness (Romans 10:10, 2 Corinthians 5:21).

9. Daniel 11:32 tells us that "The people that do know their God shall be strong and do exploits." I can do exploits for I know my God who makes me strong!

10. "His divine power hath given us all things that pertain to life and godliness" (2 Peter 1:3). I can enjoy *all things* that pertain to both life and godliness, and I can do all things through Christ Who strengthens me!

Chapter Twelve

IT CAN HAPPEN TO YOU

You don't have to be "somebody special" to receive a healing miracle. God is no respecter of persons. What He will do for one person, He will do for another. What Jesus will do for somebody else, He will do for you. In this chapter, I want to share with you healing miracles that have resulted from the use of Jesus' name, in order to strengthen your faith to receive *your* miracle.

The second great benefit of the Lord is His healing power. "Jesus Christ the same, yesterday, and today, and forever" (Hebrews 13:8). The Christ of the Gospel still heals today. I know: I have been healed by Christ; I have witnessed thousands of others who have also been healed.

I know there is a great deal of controversy on the subject of healing from Christ. There always has been, and probably there always will be. The skeptics and rank doubters deny Christ performs miracles of healing today. But those of us who have believed and received, know Christ still performs vital miracles today in this generation.

My own mother's healing was the first one to make an impact upon my life. That was in 1948, and it brought my family to Jesus. Then the Lord healed my baby daughter's clubbed feet and raised up my own sweetheart, my wife, in 1953, when she was stricken with rheumatic fever.

The name of Jesus is the healing name. When we invoke His name in ministry to the sick, it is the same as if Jesus Himself were present. He and His name are one. When the revelation of the power of Jesus' name came to my life, I was changed for life, and life was changed for me. It was as though heaven suddenly came into my life.

As I have already mentioned, in the name of Jesus I have commanded deaf spirits to leave hundreds of people who were totally deaf in one or both ears. Almost every time, the deafness has departed and the people have been healed.

Coming against the cursed disease of cancer many times, I have spoken in the authoritative name of Jesus against this foul oppression and many testimonies have been received from those healed miraculously of cancer. These healings have been real, definite miracles for the glory and praise of His name.

I have written on the flyleaf of my Bible these words: "I do not need faith to use the name of Jesus; all I need is *boldness* to use this name that belongs to me."

It has been simply wonderful to speak in the name

of Jesus against all manner of diseases, bondages, and problems, and see the results. This name of Jesus belongs to you also. Use it boldly! You may tremble when you use the name, but remember that the power is in that name, and be fearless! I bless the Lord Who healeth all our diseases!

"And his name, through faith in his name, hath made this man strong, whom ye see and know: yea, the faith which is by him hath given him this perfect soundess in the presence of you all" (Acts 3:16).

David says, "Bless the Lord, who redeemeth thy life from destruction." This means He preserves us from destruction. I am sure every one of us has been very close to the jaws of death, but the Lord's big hand has delivered us and preserved us when the evil one wanted to destroy us.

One time, I was preaching in the city of Chicago. The Lord was giving us many souls and great miracles of healing in each service. A Satan-controlled man came to the meetings. He wouldn't submit himself for deliverance, refusing the grace and mercy of God for his sin-benighted soul. He went out many times worse than he came in, because of resisting the Spirit.

Later, as I was going to the auditorium for our next meeting, this man was laying wait for me. With the sudden fierceness of a wild animal, he attacked me. Before I knew what was happening, he had struck me three damaging blows to the face. I stood there, reeling and rocking, trying to regain my equilibrium.

"I will cut your eyes out!" screamed the man, and began his uncanny approach towards me again. I knew there was no human reason for this man to attack me: I had tried to help him; but I saw that demons were clearly controlling him. As he made his approach again with the intent to cut my eyes out, I cried out in the name of Jesus, forbidding him to work further destruction.

The demons in the man were subdued. He suddenly turned and fled from the scene of violence. The name of Jesus had conquered. The Lord had redeemed my life from destruction. I bless His name for that with all that is within me.

Once I was in a critical car accident: one of the cars rolled over an embankment, and I was trapped inside with gas streaming down upon me. Unable to free myself, I quickly perceived that the raw gas could ignite and it would be a living inferno inside that car.

Again I used the name of Jesus in my dilemma and began to praise the Lord for my deliverance. The Lord undertook; six men came along and lifted the car, and I was freed from the wreck that Satan had intended would destroy me.

Hallelujah! God is bigger than the devil! And I bless the Lord Who redeemed my life from destruction! "Bless the Lord, O my soul, and ALL that is within me." All that is within me says, "Hallelujah; thank You, Jesus, praise the Lord, glory to God!" My cup runneth over! The Lord has blessed me with His benefits—I am thankful.

You can know the same benefits of the Lord that I know, if you believe in Jesus Christ. What He has done for me and many others, He will do for you.

When I was a missionary-evangelist to Dominica,

my mission was characterized by some unusual interventions of God that are deeply etched in my memory.

We went out to a Dominican village to visit the people there. Missionaries agreed to take us to the village to meet those who were ardent listeners to my broadcasts in English and French, as this was primarily a French and Patois-speaking village. The people received me warmly as God's servant as we went from one little house to the next to share with them the love of Jesus. Then I was asked to conduct an open-air service before I returned to the capital city.

As we were crossing over a bridge to conduct the open-air service on the other side of the river, a large number of school children came running towards us. They asked if they could sing a song for our party in their Patois dialect; they did so sweetly. Then they asked if we would sing a song for them; we joined them in singing "Hallelujah!" Afterwards, I told them I wanted to pray for all of them so that they would receive Jesus Christ into their hearts, and that He would bless them.

My daughter Marisa accompanied us on this journey. Marisa was not yet fifteen years of age then. She was a slim girl who was not accustomed to the tropical climate. While I was in the midst of my prayer, Marisa fainted. Had not my wife grabbed her suddenly, she might have toppled into the swift river below. As it was, she fell down to the rocks next to the river. I quickly jumped down to Marisa's side. Her eyes had rolled back in her head; there was no life, no response at all. My wife screamed, "Oh Daddy, pray!"

I didn't want to make a theological decision how I should minister to her: I heard the Spirit of the Lord praying through me, "Death, I rebuke you in Jesus' name!"

I picked Marisa up and lifted her back onto the bridge. Her eyes were still set in the backs of her eye sockets, and she was lying lifelessly in my arms as I carried her across the bridge. Again I rebuked the devil and strongly commanded: "I rebuke you, death, in the name of Jesus."

Halfway across the bridge, Marisa's eyes opened and our hearts rejoiced. We put her in the car belonging to the missionaries, Brother and Sister Snyder, and returned back to the city of Roseau. The Snyders requested us to have Marisa examined; however, we were confident the Lord had ministered to her completely. When the devil meant destruction, God wrought His miracle! I'm not claiming that Marisa was raised back from the dead but I *am* stating that the Lord intervened and touched my daughter. Praise His Name!

Many years ago Mrs. Mary Hart, of Calgary, Alberta, was traveling by horse-and-wagon across the prairies, en route to Alberta. She was just a girl then, but she remembers a particular experience vividly.

One evening, when her family made camp on the prairie, she was standing near the camp-fire. A can of boiling water suddenly exploded and the impact of the explosion badly burned her face. In time the burns were healed, but Mary was left without her sense of smell. Through the years that followed, she was deprived of the ability to smell though she was a lover of beautiful flowers.

When I conducted a four-week's crusade in Calgary, God mightily manifested His power to heal and deliver. One night, Mrs. Hart stood before me to relate her story, and to ask for prayer for healing and restoration of her sense of smell. When I ministered to her in the name of Jesus, instantly she received this miracle of healing, and was able to smell anything and everything, including flowers!

A few nights after this miracle happened, a severe electrical storm struck Calgary. Unknown to Mrs. Hart, her gas furnace pilot-light was extinguished by the force of the storm. When the pilot-light went out, the gas was supposed to cut off automatically; this did not happen, and for hours gas came whizzing from the furnace throughout the basement and upstairs. When Mrs. Hart arrived home that night from our service, she was aware that some peculiar odor was in the house everywhere. She went downstairs and quickly discovered what had happened. Opening windows and doors, she got the gas outside. Often she has given testimony that, without doubt, receiving her sense of smell was a life-saver to her! Had she not been able to smell, the gas could have continued to fill the house, and eventually would have killed her!

Yes, the can of boiling water on that open prairie fire many years ago caused young Mary to lose her sense of smell. But through the mighty name of

Jesus, God wrought a wonderful miracle that saved her life in Calgary.

Some years ago, my family and I went to North Battleford, Saskatchewan, to conduct a crusade at the Foursquare Gospel Church. The pastor, George Belobaba, challenged me with these words:

"Brother Gossett, in our Sunday School we have two children, both of whom are totally blind in one eye. Now if the Lord would grant miracles and open their eyes and give them sight, it would really stir things here, and cause people to know that Jesus Christ is alive and doing business today."

"I have seen Jesus Christ open blind eyes many times," I replied. "Let's believe that the Lord will grant these miracles when we pray for the children."

The third night of the meetings, Michael Mannix and Linda Girard attended the meetings. Pastor Belobaba pointed out these children to me and told me that they were the ones each of whom had a blind eye. I ministered to Michael, and Jesus Christ gave him perfect sight; then Linda received the same wonderful miracle.

These miracles stirred the hearts of many people, and scores of souls were attracted to the meetings and saved because of these demonstrations of the power of the living God. Michael and Linda were back night after night; I would bring them to the platform, and demonstrate how completely Jesus Christ had brought sight to eyes that were totally blind.

The miracles also had great impact upon their families: I had a letter from Linda's grandmother,

Mrs. Teichroeb; she wrote, "Not only was my granddaughter, Linda Girard, healed of the blind eye in your crusade, but two of my brothers were saved in the meetings, and I was healed of severe abdominal pains. I'm so thankful for all the Lord has done."

Michael Mannix had an older brother, Melvin, who had severe rheumatic fever which had so affected his heart that often he could not walk, talk, nor recognize his mother. When I ministered to him, Jesus Christ instantly healed him. When his mother took him for a complete examination, his doctor was amazed; he took Melvin off the medications, and pronounced him every whit whole.

In John 14:13-14, Jesus said, "Whatsoever ye shall ask in my name, that will I do, that the Father may be glorified in the Son. If ye shall ask any thing in my name, I will do it." One night in Anderson, Missouri, they brought a lady who was dying with cancer. She looked pitiful, hardly more than skin and bones; her skin was discoloured.

I asked her, "Do you believe this 'whatsoever' of John 14:13 includes your cancerous body?"

She feebly said, "Yes."

"Then let us take that big word 'whatsoever' for the cancers," I continued. "Jesus said, if you ask in my name, I will do it. It is simply reduced to this: our part is to do the asking and Jesus will take care of the doing."

The Word of God brought active faith to her heart

128

and with real assurance she exclaimed, "That sounds good to me!"

In that name of Jesus, we cursed the cancers and within three days' time they had all passed from her body. She was restored to complete health and the last account I had, she is still strong today. I exalt this name of Jesus! In the name of Jesus, we have seen practically every known disease and affliction healed except leprosy. (And I believe leprosy too will submit to this imperial name of Jesus, when we get a chance to pray for a leper!)

"In my name shall they cast out devils; they shall speak with new tongues; they shall take up serpents; and if they drink any deadly thing, it shall not hurt them; they shall lay hands on the sick, and they shall recover (Mark 16:17-18).

YOU HAVE THE ANOINTING

1. "The anointing which ye have received of Him abideth in you," (1 John 2:27). You have the anointing within you. This is a Bible fact that reads the same every day.

2. "And the yoke shall be destroyed because of the anointing," (Isaiah 10:27). The yoke speaks of satanic bondage. The anointing destroys the yoke!

3. What is the anointing? It is that supernatural, energizing force within that makes the Spirit-filled life forcible, effective and productive in Christian service. If you have received the baptism of the Holy Spirit, you have received the anointing and it abides within you!

4. Jesus our Master was the Anointed One as He walked this earth: "The Spirit of the Lord is upon Me, because He hath anointed Me to preach the gospel to the poor; He hath sent Me to heal the brokenhearted; to preach deliverance to the captives, and recovering of sight to the blind; to set at liberty them that are bruised; to preach the acceptable year of the Lord," (Luke 4:18-19). All of the healings and deliverances of Jesus were wrought by this anointing. "God anointed Jesus of Nazareth with the Holy Ghost and with power: who went about doing good, and healing all that were oppressed of the devil; for God was with Him," (Acts 10:38).

5. Treasure this anointing. It is the holy, super quality that makes us dynamic for our Lord. This anointing enables us to see Jesus-like results in our lives. This anointing gives us authority to speak in the name of Jesus against satanic powers.

6. "I shall be anointed with fresh oil," (Psalm 92:10). The anointing of the Holy Spirit is akin to oil. The Scriptures give oil as a type of the Holy Spirit. Utter these sacred words with David: "I shall be anointed with fresh oil!" On the Day of Pentecost they were all filled with the Holy Ghost (Acts 2:4); later, these same disciples were again filled with the Holy Ghost (Acts 4:29-31). We need fresh anointings and re-fillings of the Spirit.

7. "But ye, beloved, building up yourselves on your most holy faith, praying in the Holy Ghost," (Jude 20). This "praying in the Holy Ghost" is real, fervent, anointed praying that builds up our faith.

8. "But ye have an unction from the Holy One," (1 John 2:20). I covet this anointing, this unction that abides within me. Daily I yield to the Holy Spirit to impart fresh oil within my being. I confess, "I have the anointing. It abides within me. It's the gift of God. I maintain the anointing by a life of rich fellowship with my Lord."

Chapter Thirteen

THE CURE FOR CANCER

Healing belongs to us. It isn't something that we have to beg God for, it is something He has already given to us. But faith is the catalyst. Without faith in what He says, we will be unable to claim the healing that is ours by right.

Many years ago, an Englishman named William F. Burton founded the Belgian Congo Mission. This mission opened a mighty witness for Christ in Africa.

Mr. Burton became ill, but he was unaware of either the extent or the seriousness of what he had. Doctors in the Congo, now known as Zaire, prepared to operate on him. During the operation, the surgeon found that William Burton was completely filled with cancer.

His surgeon—who was also a friend of his—broke the news to Mr. Burton. "We are sorry that there is nothing we can do for you," he told Burton sadly.

132

"The cancer is too widespread. We cannot even try a radical operation to try to remove the cancer. We feel that you should know that you only have about a year to live. If you would like to return to England to see your family, you should plan to do so as soon as you are strong enough to make the trip."

William Burton agreed to wait a month or so before he returned to England. He had lived so long in the Congo and he loved the people of the Congo so deeply that he dreaded leaving. He planned to travel over the land he loved so dearly to say good-bye to his friends.

Everywhere he went, the sad news of his illness and his imminent departure had preceded him. Tearfully, his Congolese friends did their best to express their love and sympathy for him.

One evening, as was his custom, Burton was sitting in his bedroom, reading his Bible. He was reading from Isaiah 53 when the words, "with his stripes we are healed," leaped from the page to save his life. Aware that up to this point he had failed to consider the plan that *God* might have for his life, Mr. Burton dropped to his knees and prayed for forgiveness for having given way to immediate acceptance of the surgeon's decree. He himself had failed to use the Word. The words he had been repeating to himself had not been words of victory through Jesus. They had been the words of the surgeon. He decided to ask God to have the "final verdict" in his case.

After that, when Burton's Congolese friends tried to console him, he would simply say, "But you haven't heard the last of it. By his stripes I am healed." Over and over, he affirmed and reaffirmed his faith by the words he spoke. William Burton had decided to believe God.

Mr. Burton continued his plans to return to England. His reason for going now, however, was not to bid his family farewell. Instead, he planned to rest and recover his strength, so that he would be able to return to the Congo and continue the Lord's work. When his family and friends met him sorrowfully, he courageously continued his stand: "By his stripes I am healed."

About six months after Burton's return to England, when there seemed to be an improvement in his health instead of the expected deterioration, Burton's English doctors decided to examine him again. They had received his medical record from the Congo.

To the amazement of the physicians and everybody else except Mr. Burton, the examination confirmed Burton's own statement, "By his stripes I am healed." He was right. His statement was heaven's verdict in his case. Absolutely not one trace of cancer remained!

William Burton's healing had far-reaching effects. He returned to his mission in the Belgian Congo and continued his work there for many years. His healing witnessed to the Africans in a more powerful way than all his preaching had before.

The stripes that Jesus suffered for our healing were made by a type of cruel punishment called "scourging." Historians tell us that they were inflicted by what was known as a cat-o'-nine-tails.

This scourging of Jesus took place shortly before his crucifixion (Matthew 27:26).

A cat-o'-nine-tails is a horrible weapon for punishment. Little pieces of metal are woven into each one of the thongs. The Roman scourging with this whip surpassed all other methods of punishment. It was, if possible, worse than being nailed to a cross and left to die. It was so frightful that the condemned one often died while being beaten.

They tied our Savior's hands high above His head. Then a powerful Roman soldier, with all the strength he had, lashed Jesus with that whip. Thirty-nine times his cat-o'-nine-tails gouged our Lord's flesh so that His ribs and the bones of his back were exposed.

In those thirty-nine lashes which cut His back to ribbons, Jesus took unto Himself *our* misery, *our* pain, and *our* sicknesses. He suffered the agony of every known disease. He suffered so that the suffering of each one of us might be relieved, so that we might be able to say, "With his stripes I am healed."

This healing is not something that will come about if you say the words, or if you pray. It is something that has *already* been done! Just as you were saved the minute you accepted Jesus' atonement on the cross, so you can be healed the minute you really see that Jesus has already paid the price for your healing.

The scourging and crucifixion of Jesus was not pretty. It was inhumane; it might be termed bestial. What we should always realize, however, is that from early in His life, Jesus knew what His end on this earth would be. Yet He loved us so much that He walked unfalteringly toward the cross so that we who belong to Him might be able to say again and again that "By his stripes I am healed."

Henry Gallers of Wanganui, New Zealand, related this poignant account to me recently when I was overseas conducting crusades:

"On April 25, 1952, some believers were having a tarrying meeting in Wanganui. This kind of meeting often follows a formal kind of meeting. The emphasis of the ministry that evening had concerned the Holy Spirit. It had been brought out that there is no teacher so powerful as the Holy Spirit. He alone searches out the deep things of God and reveals them to us.

"A young lad of fifteen had received the Holy Spirit, and joy filled the congregation. As his mother looked at the boy, however she was disturbed. He seemed anything but joyous. His face looked pained and drawn and white. She wondered at his unusual appearance.

"Later that boy explained to us what had been happening with him. As he had been thinking of the great sacrifice that Jesus had made for him, he had had a vision of the scourging of Jesus. That's why he wasn't so joyful. He saw our Lord tied up, hanging by the wrists, suspended so that His feet just touched the ground. He saw the Roman soldier inflict on Jesus the first blow with that whip.

"That young man, like many other people, had had the idea that because Jesus was meek, he must have been a rather frail-looking, slightly-built man!

Not at all! The miles that Jesus strode over those hot, dusty Galilean hills demanded a strong and able body. Also, sometimes people forget that Jesus was only thirty-three when He was crucified. In his vision, the lad saw Jesus' young back and his massive and muscular shoulders, muscular enough to enable Him to carry that heavy cross. No matter how strong His body, however, that cat-o'-nine-tails cut Him and pained Him just as it would either you or me. The Roman soldier's lash cut a deep furrow across Jesus' back that day. It chopped his flesh and scattered blood. But Jesus was able to bear it.

"The lad's previous knowledge of the scourging of Jesus had been very limited. When he knelt to pray, he hadn't really had any idea of what a scourging was like. Unexpectedly, though, right before his closed eyes came a symbolic vision of what had happened on the spiritual level those centuries ago.

"In his mind's eye, he saw a great mob of people standing around. It was not a mob such as had actually witnessed that flogging in Jerusalem. Rather, he saw standing there a great crowd of cripples and ailing people. Some had crutches. Some had other means of support. He saw only one of the thirty-nine blows our Lord received. But as the whip recoiled from that cutting blow, pieces of flesh and flecks of blood flew out over the mob. Miracle of miracles, and with all glory to God, anywhere that the tiniest particle of flesh or the merest fleck of blood fell, the person upon whom it landed was instantly healed; he was made perfectly whole!

"The people were dropping their crutches and walking about, demonstrating their healings. Here was the Body broken, and here was the Blood shed for their healing.

"The smallest imaginable droplet of blood from that blow was charged with the power to heal. When you know that Jesus bore not one, but thirty-nine, stripes and you know the suffering that He endured, you can realize the healing power which will *yet* flow for all who will only say and mean, 'With His stripes I am healed.' The lad's vision was symbolic. The crowd he saw wasn't the crowd that actually witnessed Jesus' flogging. *We* were among the ill and crippled healed by His stripes.

"When the lad rose to his feet, joy flooded his face. He no longer dwelt on the blood and the open wounds of Jesus. He dwelt on the love that Jesus has for us; for in permitting His blood to pour out, He made healing available to all of us."

Some people may think that I overemphasize the quotation, "By His stripes I am healed," but about this, I know two things: first, this is what the Bible says; and, second, if you are God's child, you must say what the Bible says in order to get the results the Bible promises. You must put your belief into words. Since Jesus cared so much for me that He submitted to that cruel flogging and then gave His body to hang for me on that crude cross on the hillside at Calvary, I have decided to follow Him. I know that such following will lead me not only here for a short time, but, more importantly, for the hereafter in all of eternity. I am bought and paid for with that blood, and so are you.

You must develop a habit of quoting God's Word. This way of speaking will become a life habit for you. The Holy Spirit will live each day in you. God's grace will become evident in your life. And it will lead to spectacular results.

Recently Mr. and Mrs. Jens Jensen, formerly pastors in Linn Grove, Iowa, related this testimony to me:

"One afternoon the three of us, we and our fourteen-year-old daughter, were sitting in our living room, talking about the goodness of God and worshipping Him aloud as we talked.

"Esther was sitting in her wheelchair. She had suffered with tuberculosis of the bone for two years. Open sores from her ankle to her thigh exposed the bone in places. She had been in bed for over a year and had often broken out in sores in places all over her body. Now, in a temporary remission, she seemed somewhat better and was able to be up in her chair for most of the day.

"That day we were not really praying for Esther's recovery, although we had prayed for it many times in the past. We were just telling the Lord again how happy we were that we were privileged to belong to Him. Without planning to do so, we were led to approach Esther's chair and place our hands on her head. That afternoon the Holy Spirit was so real to all of us that we could feel His presence there. We just felt that something wonderful was happening in all our lives.

"From that afternoon, we began to witness a continuous change in Esther. She was not dramatically healed, but God certainly undertook her healing. The sores began to heal until gradually they were all closed. Finally, she was able to leave her chair and walk around our home. Then, to the glory of God, came the day when she could completely discard any support and take her place again in the normal activities of a teen-age girl. The scars are still there to remind us of God's mercy, but today Esther is strong, happily married, and the mother of our two grandchildren. Do you wonder that we unceasingly praise the Lord!"

How God loves to hear us say the words that reflect His goodness to us and declare our allegiance to Jesus Christ, our Lord and Savior.

You may read the great truths of the Word, truths that promise that health and healing can be yours. You may say, "I believe that they are true." But you must claim these promises for *yourself* and act upon them and talk about them, in order to benefit from them.

God put your diseases upon Jesus, "Who his own self bore our sins in his own body on the tree, that we, being dead to sins, should live unto righteousness: by whose stripes ye were healed" (1 Peter 2:24). He says, "ye *were* healed." Past tense. You have already *been* healed. So, then, you don't own illness, you own health. It's not *your* arthritis, for example, any longer. It's the *devil's* arthritis! Satan brought sin and sickness into this world, but he must yield to the authority of the name of Jesus, and the sickness must go. He can't put his sickness on you any longer.

Provided you are a born-again believer, you can truthfully say, "By his stripes I am healed."

WHAT TO DO AFTER HANDS ARE LAID ON YOU

1. You've acted on Jesus' words: "And these signs shall follow them that believe . . . they shall lay hands on the sick, and they shall recover" (Mark 16:17-18). You, as a believer, may have laid your own hands upon yourself for healing, or another believer may have laid hands upon you for your healing. In either case, you can have great assurance that there will be a performance of what Jesus has promised, for He watches over His Word to do it. This is a very positive promise: you will recover. Jesus did not say, "You might recover," or "Hope that you will recover," or "Recovery is possible." No! Without reservation, Jesus declared, "You will recover!" Praise the Lord that you are now recovering!

2. If you have not received an instantaneous miracle, do not cast away your confidence. When Jesus walked this earth, He healed people in various ways: many were healed instantly; others were healed gradually. Whether you are healed instantly or a gradual mending process has begun, you can go your way praising Him with confidence that He is keeping His Word with you.

3. Begin to confess your healing. "I am recovering. Jesus said so and I believe His Word. I am not going on how I look, how I feel, or how others think I look. I have accepted Jesus' Word at face value: I am recovering."

4. James, chapter one, declares that when you ask God for anything, you must ask in faith, nothing wavering. "For he that wavereth . . . let not that man think that he shall receive any thing from the Lord." *Any thing* includes healing. Your role in this drama of faith is to possess unwavering confidence that the Lord will keep His Word. If you waver in your faith, then you deny yourself the Lord's healing. Do not waver in your confession of faith. Confess that "By His stripes I am healed."

5. Until your healing is fully manifested, you will be engaged in a fight of faith. It is not a fight against God or His Word, but a fight against the thief who came to "kill, steal and destroy" you (John 10:10). In this conflict, use the weapons of your warfare which are mighty through God to the pulling down of satanic strongholds. Confess boldly, unwaveringly, "By His stripes I am healed!"

6. Act like you are recovering. Begin to do things you could not do before. Praise the Lord that you are recovering. When others enquire about your condition, simply share with them the fact that you are recovering, because Jesus said so.

7. The devil doesn't want you to recover. Here's how to deal with him: "Satan, I resist you in the name of Jesus, for it is written, "they shall lay

hands on the sick, and they shall recover." In Jesus' mighty name, I am recovering!"

8. God is no respecter of persons. Thousands of people have been healed through the ministry of laying on of hands. What God has done for others, He is doing for you! Praise Him now for your recovery!

Chapter Fourteen

HOW NOT TO GET WHAT YOU SAY

I recall a time early in my ministry when my prayers went unanswered, when the flow of the Spirit was clearly not manifested. I discovered that this had happened because I had allowed spiritual blockades to exist within me, and these were preventing the action of the Holy Spirit.

My problem was a very serious one. An older minister had seemingly set out to destroy my ministry. He caused me one heartache after another, hurling false accusations at me and spreading untrue tales about me. I was completely miserable.

One day a minister friend came to see me. "Don," he said, "I can see what these accusations are doing to you and your ministry. I'm going to give you this check, and I want you to use this money to publish a retaliation to the untrue charges that man is making against you. He is *ruining* you."

I agreed. For several days I worked at writing a

retaliation which would openly reveal that man for what he was, a liar and a false accuser, a ruiner of character. During the entire time that I was inwardly railing at that minister, trying to get down on paper statements that would vindicate me, I was in a turmoil. I had no peace. Even my prayers seemed from my lips and not from my heart.

Finally, I broke under the load of those wrong spirits. I met God in a time of heartfelt prayer as I confessed that it was not the Holy Spirit working in my life during those days when I was seeking personal retribution. I prayed for the Holy Spirit to guide me through that darkness.

The Holy Spirit showed me that I had been wrong. Then my attitude changed. Instead of hating that man and trying to get even with him, I was filled anew by the Holy Spirit. I discovered that the Holy Spirit had ministered God's love to my heart. Filled with God's love, I could think clearly and see that man through God's eyes of kindness, forgiveness, even tenderness. This was one of the greatest supernatural experiences I ever had: the Spirit of the Lord enabled me to forgive that man completely, when I, without the Spirit, hated him, wanted to get even with him, and had every reason to feel bad.

The Bible tells us that vengeance is God's business: "Avenge not yourselves, but rather give place unto wrath: for it is written, Vengeance is mine; I will repay, saith the Lord" (Romans 12:19). God takes vengeance on our enemies because He is just, and because He loves us. However, an unforgiving spirit is so destructive that we are warned that when God *does* take vengeance on our enemies, we are not even to be happy that He did so! "Rejoice not when thine enemy falleth, and let not thine heart be glad when he stumbleth: Lest the Lord see it, and it displease him and he turn away his wrath from him" (Proverbs 24:17-18).

During the time that I was planning to refute the minister who had wronged me, I was disobeying Jesus' command to "Resist not evil; but whosoever shall smite thee on thy right cheek, turn to him the other also" (Matthew 5:39). But not only was I disobeying one of God's express commands, I was also making it impossible for Him to forgive me, since "If ye forgive men their trespasses, your heavenly Father will also forgive you: But if ye forgive not men their trespasses, neither will your Father forgive your trespasses" (Matthew 6:14, 15). No wonder my prayers were being hindered! This is why Jesus said, "And when ye stand praying, forgive, if ye have aught against any: that your Father also which is in heaven may forgive you your trespasses" (Mark 11:25).

Hatred, anger, envy, unforgiveness, and like emotions hurt us more than they hurt the one who has wronged us. This is because, if our faith is strong and our prayer is persistent, there is only one thing that can stand in the way of answered prayer, and that is unrepented sin. Isaiah 59:1, 2 says, "Behold, the LORD's hand is not shortened that it cannot save; neither his ear heavy, that it cannot hear: but your iniquities have separated between you and your God, and your sins have hid his face from you, that he will not hear." What a terrible condition for a Christian to be in—to be unable to talk to God!

When we understand what our resentment does to us, we see how much better it is for us to allow our enemies to get away with murder and forgive them, rather than hold a grudge and cut ourselves off from God. God knows our enemy's heart—if the hurt was intentional, God will repay.

Once you understand the destructiveness of "getting even," you will be able to ask God to keep you from resentment in all its forms. That it is possible to be truly free from these feelings I know not only from my own experience, but also from Scripture. In Acts 13 we have the account of two of God's steadfast servants, both Spirit-filled men. Paul and Barnabas were preaching and teaching in Antioch. Paul told the gentiles there that he and Silas had come to Antioch because God had sent them there to be a light to them, that salvation might be brought to the uttermost parts of the earth. When the gentiles heard that, they were glad and they glorified God, and all those who believed received the Spirit and were ordained to eternal life. The Jews, however, incited the devout men and women against Paul and Barnabas and drove them from the city. Paul and Barnabas left, and *they were filled with joy in the Holy Spirit!*

Paul and Barnabas had no desire for retaliation. The Spirit-filled life doesn't seek that, but joyously reflects the presence of God within instead. Paul's words were bold for Christ. Because he spoke those words, he was met with disdain and rebuff. He knew, however, that the Holy Spirit had promised power, so he never hesitated to speak the Word. This is what will happen with you, as the Spirit fills you.

HOW TO OVERCOME
UNFORGIVENESS

Make this a personal confession of faith. What you confess, you'll possess. When you say what God says about this vital subject, you'll possess what He has provided for you: the divine ability to forgive everyone.

1. If I forgive men their trespasses against me, my heavenly Father will also forgive me my trespasses against Him (Matthew 6:14). But if I forgive not men their trespasses against me, far more serious consequences than I had imagined will be mine: "Neither will your heavenly Father forgive you your trespasses" (Matthew 6:15).

2. If I possess unforgiveness in my heart towards others, regardless of their wrong doings against me, I open my heart to permit seven other spirits more wicked than unforgiveness to enter in (Luke 11:26). Here are seven other spirits which are akin to unforgiveness but are even more wicked:
   Resentment.
   Ill-will.
   A grudge.
   Malice.
   Retaliation.
   Bitterness.
   Hatred.

3. As I examine this list of seven other spirits more wicked than unforgiveness, I perceive that they are progressively degrading. How can I be delivered from unforgiveness? How can I resist these wrong spirits in Jesus' name, that they must leave me? I can "be...kind one to another, tender-hearted, forgiving one another, even as God for Christ's sake, hath forgiven" me (Ephesians 4:32). Kindness is a fruit of the Spirit, which when coupled with tenderheartedness, enables me to forgive all who have wronged me, even as God for Christ's sake has forgiven me.

4. If I have a quarrel with anyone, I must forgive him. Even as Christ has forgiven me, I also forgive others (Colossians 3:13). God's Word is so practical and powerful: it shows me what to do even if I should be involved in a petty quarrel.

5. God's ability within me to forgive others is unlimited. Jesus has commanded me to forgive even "seventy times seven" times, meaning that I possess, not natural ability, but supernatural ability, whereby I can forgive others.

6. The greatest problems I encounter in life may well be "people problems." I live in a world where communications can break down; fellowship may be severed; persecution and

opposition may be my lot. But I know the secret. I have the ability to love with God's love. His love will enable me to see others through eyes of tender love and compassion.

7. I refuse to speak unkindly against those who have wronged me. God enables me to forgive and to forget. "Seven other spirits" may often seek to gain entrance to my life, but I defiantly resist them in Jesus' name!

8. Some say, "I would forgive others if they would only ask me for forgiveness." Whether they ever ask for forgiveness or not, in my heart of hearts, I forgive and put all offenses under the Blood of Jesus. As a Jesus person I forgive others. By the delivering power of the Blood of Jesus, I am free from "seven other spirits."

Chapter Fifteen

START TALKING!

Some years ago I was in Asia, working among the Moslems there. I was trying to turn their lives around toward Jesus Christ. I was explaining to them that Jesus is the *living* Son of God, that He is the only means by Whom mankind can be saved. My whole heart was in my work there. I was trying hard to walk each day with God and to please Him, yet everything seemed so difficult for me. One block after another appeared in my path. The work did not seem to be going forward.

One day a cablegram came from my wife in Canada. To add to my problems there in Asia, the cablegram held very discouraging personal news. I desperately needed God to undertake the clearing away of all those obstacles that only He could understand. While our human understanding of an entire situation is always limited to our own narrow view of the picture and our limited perception of what is happening, God, the Omniscient One, is seeing all of it! He knew what was happening in Asia. He knew what was happening in my family in Canada.

I had to talk to God. I asked Him to come to the foreground and to put me into the background. *I* had no answers to the many problems that confounded me. My prayers *did* get results. My own life quieted as I trusted God to straighten out the problems in my family and to deal with my limitations in trying to reach the Moslems. And He did.

A few days ago among my papers, I found the notebook in which I had written my basis for prayer as I prepared to present to my Heavenly Father the desperate need I had at that time. I had written from Psalm 116:1, "I love the Lord, because he hath heard my voice."

How do *you* feel when you love someone you know? If you were forbidden ever to talk to that person, how sad you would be! If the restriction were lifted and you were again permitted to talk with him, how delighted you would be! That is exactly what our relationship is with God, if we truly love Him. If we do love Him, we want to talk with Him. We want to seek His help in our lives. We want Him to *know* how much we love Him, just as we want our earthly loved ones to know that we love *them*. We want to give Him gifts, as we want to give gifts to our earthly loved ones. We want to tell others of His wonderful qualities, as we are proud to publicize the outstanding qualities of those here about whom we care. But above all, we want to be close to him, to talk to Him, to listen to Him, if we really love Him. That "talking to God" is praying.

When I was a boy, I prayed for God to keep our home together. In spite of every indication to the contrary, the Lord did just that! Our home, though often threatened by permanent breakup and divorce, was held together only by miracles of answered prayer. I prayed for the Lord to save my entire family; and they were classified by many as some of the most sin-hardened, indifferent, unresponsive, unlikely candidates who ever faced the Lord! But that is Jesus' specialty, saving sinners, just as He did my family. If the Lord by prayer saved *my* family, you can take encouragement that your family, however hard-hearted, can be won to Jesus Christ.

As a young Baptist minister, I prayed fervently that God would make me the kind of minister He wanted me to become. Little did I know that He would answer that prayer by baptizing me in the Holy Spirit and by giving me an anointed deliverance ministry in the years ahead.

I prayed for God to open doors to me for a radio ministry. He answered that prayer. He has given me the privilege and the responsibility of sharing the Gospel by air waves in eighty-nine different nations spread across the world.

How I prayed that the Lord would make me a soul-winner! I praise Him that He has answered that prayer by using me to help to turn thousands of people to Him as I have had the joy of leading them

153

to the Savior. Praise God for His wonderful answer to that prayer, for it means those additional souls will live in heaven throughout eternity!

I prayed to God to bring each of my children to a personal acceptance of Jesus Christ as Savior, and He has done that. They've all been water-baptized and baptized in the Holy Spirit.

Prayer is not only a blessed privilege, but as we learn to know Jesus, we come to realize that prayer is the vital breath of the Christian life. When breath ceases, so does life. When prayer ceases, so does the vibrancy of a Christian's spiritual life.

Some years ago, the Holy Spirit revealed to me the power and authority we have in Jesus. During that time, I was preaching daily on radio stations in Lodi and Modesto, California. It was then that I learned that Jesus has given us the right to do the works He did—in fact, He promises that we will do so! He says in John 14:12-14, "Verily, verily, I say unto you, He that believeth on me, the works that I do shall he do also; and greater works than these shall he do; because I go unto my Father. And whatsoever ye shall ask in my name, that will I do, that the Father may be glorified in the Son. If ye shall ask anything in my name, I will do it."

Through these years that have followed, I have shared with multitudes of believers our rights and privileges in claiming the authority Jesus has given us. Colossians 3:17 advises, "Whatsoever ye do in word or deed, do all in the name of the Lord Jesus, giving thanks to God and the Father by him." As we have done so, the sick have been healed. Demons have been cast out. Salvation has come to those who formerly had rejected God. And all through calling in prayer on the name of the Lord Jesus.

No *man* does these things. Only Jesus Christ can and does do these things. But He uses men as the channels through which the words go out to turn others to Him. Words effect these miracles by Christ. When we encounter any of these seemingly unalterable, insufferable conditions in living, we perceive the tragedy present in those lives. We are moved by the Holy Spirit to be concerned. We meditate. We believe. We talk to God. We go to His throne in prayer, our words based on our belief that God is listening and that He will answer. Our words go out, seeking help for ourselves and for others in need of God's healing of our spirits, our minds, and our bodies. Jesus becomes our attorney, pleading for all mankind before God.

Logos Magazine carried a picture of Mr. and Mrs. William Hinderlider, residents of Los Angeles at the time of printing. Mr. Hinderlider serves on the board of elders of Angelus Temple in Los Angeles. He ministers to the sick in Los Angeles hospitals and to out-of-town callers from all over America. Mr. Hinderlider is now one hundred and seven years old! And he gives God all the credit for his long life in which he has been able to serve in Jesus' name. He attests to answered prayer.

T.L. Osborn, in his book *Young in Faith*, reveals some important truths about remaining fresh in our desire and ability to be on "talking terms" with God. God wants us to express our heart's desire in our prayers to Him. Oh, He *knows* what we need, but He waits for our words of acknowledgment to Him as our Lord; He waits for our expression of faith that He is able to do that which He has promised. He waits for us to "collect" on those promises.

Mr. Osborn remarks on his amazement that some people become "old"—not mature, simply "old"—in their faith at such a young physical age. Because of their lax attitude toward prayer, many middle-aged people weary in their faith. This happens because there is no infusion of the Holy Spirit, the kind of revitalizing that occurs as a person, through prayer, seeks new truth, new strength for each day, as each day he goes to God in prayer.

Mr. Osborn continues, saying that people who get answers to their prayers are people who pray. On the surface, that might seem like an obvious conclusion. What Mr. Osborn is saying, however, is that prayers without answers may be rituals. Prayers that get answers, however, are occasions of joy and blessing.

Again, the matter comes right down to our words. God is not interested in your waxing eloquent as you speak to Him, either privately or publicly. God is interested in the simplicity and honesty of your belief in Him. In Matthew 6:5-6, Jesus said, "And when thou prayest, thou shalt not be as the hypocrites are: for they love to pray standing in the synagogues and in the corners of the streets, *that they may be seen of men*. Verily, I say unto you, they *have* their reward. But thou, when thou prayest, enter into thy closet, and when thou hast shut the door, pray to thy Father which is in secret; and thy Father which seeth in secret shall reward thee openly." Jesus was saying that those who pray to be heard by men have already received their reward, for having prayed so, *they have been heard* by the men they were seeking to impress. And that's the *end* of their reward. Here, Jesus is not condemning public prayers; but He *is* saying, "Be careful of your motive when you pray."

Many years ago, I had a dear Pentecostal friend whose life was a continuous witness to the power of praise and prayer. One day, when I was depressed and feeling that I was sadly lacking spiritually, I visited her. On her wall was a beautiful motto with just two words: "Try Praise." It seemed to me exactly as though God had looked down on me in my inadequate condition and had said to me, "Don, try praising Me." Those words spoke so clearly and movingly to me!

My friend told me that the motto had meant much to her in her life. Following its directive, she had worked out a practical formula of procedure for her own problems and her times of distress and discouragement. First, she went to prayer, asking the Lord to help and to guide her. Next, she took her Bible to seek a thought that would definitely lead her in her particular difficulty. Because the Bible *is* God's Word, He often spoke to her open mind and heart through a scripture verse, giving assurance that He was working through her belief in Him. After that, she never petitioned Him again about the matter. "To keep asking each day seems like doubting Him," she said. "I just remind Him of His promise and I thank Him for the answer, already on the way."

Those words made all the difference in that dear woman's life. She kept before herself the advice of her motto, just those two words. She offered her words of petition and praise to God. Then she sought His Word on the subject. In her heart, she listened as God spoke to her from His Word. After that, she used her words only to remind God that she was patiently waiting for His will. And what she said was what she got!

It is a good thing to pray through times of difficulty, but we can also *praise* when prayer seems to be failing. Such words of praise delight God, for He knows that we are expressing our continued faith in Him and our continued reliance on Him. This was the experience of God's faithful prophet Habakkuk, for he had prayed, "O Lord, how long shall I cry, and thou wilt not hear," (Habakkuk 1:2). But when he began to praise God, he was lifted up in spirit until he was able to say, "Although the fig tree shall not blossom, neither shall fruit be in the vines; the labor of the olive shall fail, and the fields shall yield no fruit, the flock shall be cut off from the fold, and there shall be no herd in the stalls: yet I will rejoice in the Lord, I will joy in the God of my salvation" (Habakkuk 3:17-18).

Many people are expert "askers" of God, but not such successful "receivers" from God. When we ask the Father for something, we should then begin to expect the answer, even before we have seen or felt the evidence. We pray in that faith, or it is useless to pray at all, for "Faith is the substance of things *hoped for*, the evidence of things *not seen*" (Hebrews 11:1; italics added). If we could already *see* the results, that for which we had been praying, we would no longer need to be asking God. We must *believe* that God hears, even when all the things around us might be indicating differently.

If you are praying in Jesus' name and you are still not receiving answers to your prayers, not having your needs supplied, not having supernatural acts done in your behalf, it may mean that you have simply a *form* without power. Mark 11:25 warns you to come to God in prayer with love and forgiveness in your heart, "And whenever you stand praying, forgive, if you have anything against anyone, so that your Father in heaven may forgive *you* your trespasses." Do not ever seek retaliation against those who have misused you. That will block your prayers. Cleanse yourself and lift those who have mistreated you to God in your prayer. Pray for each one by his very own name, and practice words of forgiveness. As always, your words will make that forgiveness come true. What you speak often and affirm to yourself, becomes your belief. Your belief determines your acts, and they become your way of life.

Repeating the Scriptures to yourself will begin that process, but ultimately, for the fulfillment of your needs and your salvation and to give you spiritual strength for each day, you must begin talking to God. When you discover that He, above all others, is your Friend, you will never stop that conversation so long as He gives you breath with which to pray.

Those words you utter will make all the difference in the profit you begin to reap as you walk through life, talking to God!

You must ask for that which you want to get.

PRAISE THE LORD ANYHOW!

"His praise shall continually be in my mouth" (Psalm 34:1).

1. Do you feel the joy of the Lord in your soul? Praise the Lord! Or do you feel blank inside, or even worse, do you feel depressed? **Praise the Lord anyhow!** It is "the sacrifice of praise to God continually" you are commanded to offer (Hebrews 13:15). "The sacrifice of praise" means **Praise the Lord anyhow,** especially when you don't feel like it!

2. Are all your children saved? Praise the Lord! Or are some still wandering in sin? **Praise the Lord anyhow!** God promises by believing, ALL your household will be saved (Acts 16:31). Praising the Lord for their salvation, in advance of seeing them in the fold, is evidence that you truly believe!

3. Are all your bills paid up-to-date? Praise the Lord! Or are you plagued by financial problems? **Praise the Lord anyhow!** Praise activates God's promise of plenty of money to supply all your needs. Praise Him as you affirm, "My God is **now** supplying all my needs" (Philippians 4:19). Repeat it seven times, "Thank you, Father for Thy riches now."

4. Are you enjoying good health? Praise the Lord! Or are you having health problems?

Praise the Lord anyhow! Healing is received by faith, and praise is the language of faith. "As thou hast believed, so be it done unto thee" (Matthew 8:13).

5. Is the weather good, to your liking? Praise the Lord! Or is it unpleasant weather? **Praise the Lord anyhow!** "This is the day which the Lord hath made: we will rejoice and be glad in it" (Psalm 118:24).

6. Do you have true friends, who encourage you in times of testing? Then be like Paul, when he saw his friends while being taken to prison in Rome, "he thanked God and took courage" (Acts 28:15). But perhaps you are experiencing "people problems" from those who oppose you, belittle you, or disappoint you. **Praise the Lord anyhow!**

7. **Praise the Lord anyhow!** Why? "We know that all things work together for good to them that love God, to them who are called according to His purpose" (Romans 8:28). Don't miss God's plan by praising the Lord only for things you label "blessings." His command is: "In everything give thanks: for this is the will of God in Christ Jesus concerning you" (1 Thessalonians 5:18).

Chapter Sixteen

NOTHING TO FEAR BUT FEAR

Franklin Delano Roosevelt told the American people that "We have nothing to fear but fear itself." His statement has more truth in it than most people realize. Did you know that *fear* has creative power? It has the power to create the thing we fear, just as faith has the power to create the thing we believe. That is why Job said, "The thing I feared has come upon me."

All too often, the thing we fear *does* come upon us. Doctors tell us that it is often those people who *fear* cancer who *get* cancer. They explain this by saying that possibly cancer is in part psychosomatically induced—but I explain this by saying that cancer, just like everything else, follows God's laws of faith: *What You Say Is What You Get*.

If you say, "It would be just my luck to get that. My mother had it, my relatives on my father's side had that, and I'm afraid I'm going to get it," you *will* get "it"—whatever your particular "it" happens to be. This is because fear is believing something bad will happen. Fear is *believing* something bad. Fear is actually faith in something you don't want to happen. Just as we use the word "faith" to express believing in something good, we use the word "fear" to express believing in something bad. This is why fear cancels out faith, and faith cancels out fear.

In a very real way, doubt is a form of fear: it is being afraid that the thing you want won't happen. That this is so, we see from the time Peter walked on the water: Peter had asked Jesus to bid him walk on the water, and Jesus had told Peter to come to Him. Then Peter "walked on the water, to go to Jesus. But when he saw the wind boisterous, he was afraid; and beginning to sink, he cried, saying, Lord save me. And immediately Jesus stretched forth his hand, and caught him, and said unto him, O thou of little faith, wherefore didst thou doubt?" (Matthew 14:29-31). Here, Peter "was afraid," and Jesus called this "doubt."

In a special news release sent around the world on the United Press Wire Service, a leading neuro-scientist, Dr. Stuart Wolf, made this statement: "Heart attacks occur most frequently in those emotionally upset, those depressed, or those at the end of their rope, shunned by a tight society with no place to turn. Sudden death is often caused by dejection, discouragement, and overwhelming or sudden fear."

Leading doctors around the world declared in this news release that they are experimenting with devices to block these killer impulses. It is noteworthy that fear has been discovered to be a principal cause in fatal heart attacks. To reveal to you just exactly how destructive fear is, here are more words from Dr. Wolf: "Drowning victims often are found to have no water in their lungs; the patient just died of a turned-off heart as a result of fear. The same could be true of those who have died of snake bites, for it has been discovered that only about twenty percent of snake-bite deaths have had enough venom to kill the victims."

When we consider such startling facts from that honored field, medical science, we can see the folly of giving place to fear. Indeed, to possess the abundant life Jesus has provided, as well as the long, blessed life promised in the Bible, we must overcome our fears, our depressions, and our wrong mental attitudes. *That* requires some talking to ourselves. We must affirm often, "God hath not given me the spirit of fear, but of power, and of love, and of a sound mind."

In thinking of Dr. Wolf's statement about how fear can literally turn the heart off and cause instant death, I am reminded of a widespread story I heard years ago. The freshmen in a certain college were being initiated by the upper classmen. One young man was blindfolded at the school and driven by upperclassmen to the railroad yards. There he was securely tied by ropes to the train tracks, still blindfolded. In a few minutes, the evening train sounded in the distance. Telling the young man that they were leaving him there to be struck by the oncoming train, the upperclassmen left. Only they, of course, knew that the young man was tied to tracks not in use. After the train had sped by, the upperclassmen returned to the tracks, laughing and joking because of the evident fright the young man would have experienced. He, however, had not been able to *see* that the approaching train had been traveling on another set of tracks. When they arrived to untie him, to their grief and dismay, the young man was dead! Doctors exclaimed that he had literally been frightened to death! Fear had turned his heart off. He was dead.

For many years, I have been preaching, challenging Christians to live a life free from fear. I know personally the awful consequence of fearful living. I used to be a victim of fear, and I have known the torment of a fearful existence, but praise God, I have learned that faith is the antidote to fear.

Freedom from fear does not come naturally to most of us. In most cases, it is something that you have to learn. Edna M. Devin, a missionary to Asia at the time of World War II, admits how she had to learn to put her life entirely in the hands of God. This unforgettable lesson came through Samuel Schwarz, a completed Jew. This is Edna Devin's story.

"An Austrian Jew, Samuel Schwarz, while still in his teens, was led to Christ through the teachings of Presbyterian missionaries. His Orthodox family thereafter cast him out. They 'buried' him, according to Jewish custom, and from that moment, they considered him 'dead.'

"Although Samuel had thought that that would *be* his parents' position if he accepted Christ, he had hoped that he could continue to be part of the Schwarz home. Now, cast out, broken-hearted, he left Austria, for he had made his choice! It was Jesus Christ.

"He went first to England and then later to Australia, where he was filled with the Holy Spirit. During a long life of serving and giving, he had always been a faithful witness for his Lord, Jesus Christ. It was there in Australia that we missionaries met Mr. Schwarz.

"After Japan entered the war, we were bombed out of our mission. We went to Australia, where we were taken into the Schwarzes' home. We will never forget the great love and kindness heaped upon us in that home. While there with that dear man, I learned a lesson that I will never forget. Something he said one evening as we sat talking has been a blessing to me many times since.

"We were telling the Schwarzes the wonderful story of the way we had escaped capture by the Japanese when all natural hope was gone. We told them how God had given us inward peace, even when bombs dropped by enemy planes were exploding all around us, and shrapnel was falling like rain in a heavy monsoon.

"Mr. Schwarz listened as we told how we had lived through those ten days of bombings without one of us being injured. We told how God provided food for us by means of Christian friends to whom we had ministered, friends who had risked their own lives every day to help us. We told how those same friends again risked their lives to see that we were able to leave their country. We told him of the fear that we had had for our lives, minute by minute.

"Then that devout man of God said something that made an indelible impression on my mind and my heart. 'Ah, but Sister Devin, God is so much greater than our fears!' It was such a simple statement, but it contained a release from any fear that might ever attack us.

"Often in the course of our conversation while we stayed with the Schwarzes, we talked about the future of our missionary work in the light of the war conditions. When I began to feel fear for what might happen, always came Samuel Schwarz's words of faith, words that were like dew from heaven for my thirsting soul, 'Ah, God is so much greater than our fears.'

"The truth struck home. I realized that as long as I abode in God, I need not fear. We read that fear is a lack of trust in His greatness, a lack of love. According to Revelation 21:8, the fear that the *world* knows, can separate us from God. In this atomic age, the fear of what is coming upon the earth is making the hearts of many very heavy and burdened with fear. And well might one fear *outside* God.

The natural reaction of any normally healthy body is fear toward anything which causes death, hurt, or destruction. No man is born without fear. But in our Lord Jesus Christ, we find the calming of our fears as we say to ourselves, "God is so much greater than our fears." The more we love Him and the closer we stay to Him, the more we talk to Him, the less we fear. Deriving our courage from God frees our minds and spirits, and even makes our bodies function better.

There are many different types of fear, but the Bible says that "*God* hath not given us the spirit of fear." Then where does the spirit of fear come from? Who is the contradictor of God? Who is the adversary of God? Who tries to create in us all the feelings that will separate us from God and from His peace? There can be but one answer: the devil. As long as the devil can keep us from repeating those words from Isaiah 41:10, "Fear thou not, for I am with thee; be not dismayed, for I am thy God; I will keep thee; yea, I will strengthen thee; yea, I will uphold thee with the right hand of my righteousness," he holds us in bondage.

Many are oppressed by the fear of death, the fear of some disease, the fear of calamity, the fear of old age, and on and on and on: fear of every conceivable life situation. But we must realize that it is not God who has given us that spirit of fear. That comes from the devil.

Fortunately, God never leaves us without instruction and hope. His Word can free us from all our fears, whatever they may be. In 1 John 4 are words that hold the key to victory over fear: "There is no fear in love, but perfect love casts out fear." Perfect Love? Only One was Perfect Love. That was Jesus Christ: your Shepherd, your Supplier, your Defender, your Giver of Courage, your Savior! But you must say the words which will make known your choice: fear with the devil, or peace and fulfillment with God.

Recently I read in a national magazine of a

questionnaire sent to several hundred college students. The questionnaire sought to find briefly these students' thoughts on life and its meaning. Of the many answers received, sixty percent of those young people cited fear as their dominant feeling. How sad that they had never learned, "Fear not, for I am with thee."

Years ago, we had in our evangelistic party Herschel Murphy of Texas. He was not only a minister, but he was also a soloist. Anyone who ever heard him sing "Take Your Burdens to the Lord and Leave Them There," would never forget it. He had some pointed remarks to make about fear:

"As there have been in every age, today there are people who are literally 'scared to death.' Phantoms of the past haunt them, dread of the future paralyzes them, while the hopelessness of the present numbs them. They are tormented and bedeviled, harassed and vexed, oppressed and depressed, beaten down and defeated. What a destructive force is fear!

"David said, 'I will trust and not be afraid.' By their actions, many people today seem to be saying the reverse: 'I will be afraid and not trust. Surely doubts and fears shall follow me all the days of my life; I will fear all sorts of evil, for Thou art not with me.' Such people are bound hand and foot, shackled, fettered, muzzled, and hobbled by the myriad legions of fears that beset them day and night."

God is sorrowful when He sees and hears His creatures so untrusting. He is our Father. He wants to hear us saying, "I know the Source of my strength and my courage."

RESISTING THE DEVIL

James 4:7 says, "Resist the devil and he will flee from you." Here is how you can resist the devil and have daily deliverance from the devil's "Big D's," all of which can be brought on by a fearful frame of mind.

1. Detect the devil's devices.
2. Disagree with the devil by agreeing with God.
3. Use the name of Jesus. "In my name shall they cast out devils" (Mark 16:17).
4. Boldly quote the Word of God. "And they overcame him by the blood of the Lamb, and by the word of their testimony" (Revelation 12:11).

The Devil's D's

DEFEAT - "Nay, in all these things we are more than conquerors through Him that loved us" (Romans 8:37).

DISEASES - "Bless the Lord ... who healeth all thy diseases" (Psalms 103:3).

DISCOURAGEMENT - "Fear not, neither be discouraged" (Deuteronomy 1:21).

DISTRESS - "What shall we then say to these things? If God be for us, who can be against us?" (Romans 8:31).

DEBTS - "But my God shall supply all of your need according to His riches in glory by Christ Jesus" (Philippians 4:19).

DISHEARTENMENT - "Delight thyself also in the Lord, and He shall give thee the desires of thine heart" (Psalms 37:4).

DESOLATION - "None of them that trust in Him shall be desolate" (Psalms 34:22).

DESTRUCTION - "The thief cometh not, but for to steal, and to kill, and to destroy: I am come that they might have life, and that they might have it more abundantly" (John 10:10).

DEVOURING - "Your adversary the devil, as a roaring lion, walketh about, seeking whom he may devour; whom resist steadfast in the faith" (1 Peter 5:8-9).

DISAPPOINTMENT - "And we know that all things work together for good to them that love God, to them who are the called according to His purpose" (Romans 8:28).

DISHONESTY - "We have renounced the hidden things of dishonesty" (2 Corinthians 4:2).

DISSENSION - "Behold, how good and how pleasant it is for brethren to dwell together in unity" (Psalms 133:1).

DESPONDENCY - "Rejoice in the Lord always; and again I say rejoice" (Philippians 4:4).

DOUBT - "Neither be ye of doubtful mind" (Luke 12:29), "I believe God, that it shall be even as it was told me" (Acts 27:25).

Chapter Seventeen

THE MISSING PERSON

An evangelist had just concluded a service in a crusade he was conducting. Customarily, after each service, he talked with and counseled individuals who came to him with personal problems.

This particular evening, a Mrs. Meyers, the mother of two boys, came sincerely seeking help. She told the evangelist, "My two sons are not Christians. They are almost grown men, and I am so unhappy about their indifference to God. I have prayed for them for many years," she commented, "and still they are not saved. Please be honest with me and tell me why they do not come to God."

It is difficult to establish a close enough personal relationship in a very short time to answer a question of that depth, but the evangelist began to probe. "Is your husband saved?"

"Oh, yes," she answered. "He is a very good

Christian." Then he asked, "Do you have a family altar in your home?"

"Yes," came her response. "Furthermore, we say grace at every meal; we go to church every Sunday; we rarely miss a service. In spite of all this," she continued, "and in spite of my praying, my boys don't give themselves to God."

The minister realized that this woman was honestly seeking. He sensed that the lack of answer to her prayer lay basically with her and not with her boys. "Mrs. Meyers," he said after a short pause, "do you really want to know the truth? It may hurt you. Do you want me to be frank with you?"

"Yes," she replied, "I really do want to know, for this is a continuous burden in my life."

"Then I'll tell you. There is a missing Person in your life. Your boys are not saved because your eyes are dry. You cannot be the means of saving your boys. Only the third Person of the Trinity—the Holy Spirit—can do that. Before He can, you must ask Jesus to send the Holy Spirit to fill your *own* life; then, as you pray, He will speak to your boys and make them aware of the choice they must make; to live with God or to live without God."

Mrs. Meyers dropped her head and said humbly, "I know what you mean."

When she went home that night, that mother shut herself alone in her room, and for hours she paced back and forth across that room. She poured out her broken heart to God. Her words of contrition sounded aloud. "Please, God, search my heart. Forgive me for presuming that *I* could bring my boys to You. Fill me with the Holy Spirit, so that it will be

He and not I who speaks to my boys and then reveals the Truth to my two dear ones." Finally, she felt a peace that she had never before experienced.

After her own heart had been broken, she wept, realizing her own inadequacy. Then, and only then, did the Holy Spirit give her a positive prayer burden for her sons.

The next morning, she got up as usual and prepared breakfast for her husband and her two boys. Her reticence left her as, guided by the Holy Spirit, she said to her older son, as they sat there together at the breakfast table, "Ronald, I wish you would give your heart to Jesus."

Without saying a single word, he got up and left the house. Silently his mother prayed, "Now, Jesus, it is up to You. *I* can't do one thing more. I am leaving it in Your hands."

Then she turned to her younger son and said, "John, you have also been on my heart. Will you not open your heart to Christ and receive Him as your Savior today?"

John felt the change that had come over his mother. Her voice was more tender, and in it was an appeal that he had never heard before that morning. "Mother," responded John to his mother's plea, "I *want* to become a Christian. I will give my heart to Christ today." The two of them knelt side by side there in that kitchen. Mrs. Meyers poured out her heart in thanksgiving to God. John, too, prayed. Simply and earnestly he repented of his sins and accepted the Lord Jesus as his Savior. He was there born again of the Spirit of God into God's redeemed family.

This story, however, has an even happier ending. At dinner-time, Ronald, her older son, returned home. Without saying a single word, he went straight to his mother and put his arms around her. He hugged her.

Before he had a chance to speak, his mother exclaimed, "Ronald, you don't have to tell me! I know you are saved. Tell me how it happened!"

"Mother," he said, "last night after I went to bed, I was hungry. I got up to go to the refrigerator to get something to eat. When I passed your room, I heard you talking. I stopped to listen, for I was afraid there was something wrong. I heard you talking to God, and you were praying so differently. You were pleading with God to save me." He continued, quietly explaining, "I listened to your praying, and something touched my heart. I realized then how awful it is to be a sinner and not to know how to overcome that sinning. I knew then that I needed God. When you asked me this morning, I just couldn't answer you. I had to get off by myself. I went out into the field and prayed. The Lord met me there, Mother. I accepted Jesus as my Savior. He brought peace to me, and I am *sure* that I am saved."

The "Something" that touched Ronald Meyers the night he heard his mother praying was the Holy Spirit. Then the Holy Spirit used her words to move her boys toward God.

That evangelist related this story at services later in the crusade. He wanted to emphasize that Spiritless words fall on deaf ears. But when a Spirit-filled Christian asks in God's name and to His glory, power moves out through the Spirit and does not return empty.

Like Mrs. Meyers, many Christians have felt the need for more power in their witnessing and in their personal lives. Yet many churches do not teach their members how to obtain this power, although it is plainly spelled out in the Scriptures. In Acts 1:8, Jesus told his disciples that "Ye shall receive power, after that the Holy Ghost is come upon you: and ye shall be witnesses unto me both in Jerusalem, and in all Judea, and in Samaria, and unto the uttermost parts of the earth."

Before Pentecost, the Holy Spirit was with some people but not in them. Jesus told these people that "I will pray the Father, and he shall give you another Comforter, that he may abide with you for ever, even the Spirit of truth . . . ye know him; for he dwelleth with you, and shall be in you" (John 14:16-17). But "when the day of Pentecost was fully come" the Holy Spirit was made available to all believers. In the first sermon he preached after receiving the baptism of the Holy Spirit himself, Peter told a gathering of Jews that they should, "Repent, and be baptized every one of you in the name of Jesus Christ for the remission of sins, and ye shall receive the gift of the Holy Ghost. For the promise is unto you, and to your children, and to all that are afar off, even as many as the Lord our God shall call" (Acts 2:38-39).

Many people think of the baptism of the Holy Spirit as something they can earn, by being good. According to Scripture, however, it is a gift of God, available to any Christian who asks God for it, just like salvation. As Jesus put it, "If a son shall ask bread of any of you that is a father, will he give him a stone? or if he ask a fish, will he for a fish give him a serpent? Or if he shall ask an egg, will he offer him a scorpion? If ye then, being evil, know how to give good gifts unto your children: how much more shall your heavenly Father give the Holy Spirit to them that ask him?" (Luke 11:11-13).

Other people think that because they are Christians, they automatically have the Holy Spirit, and they *do* have Him. But with the baptism of the Holy Spirit, they will receive still more of Him. We know of at least one instance after Pentecost where born-again believers had not received the baptism in the Holy Spirit simultaneously with conversion and they needed—like many modern-day believers—to receive it as a second experience: "Now when the apostles which were at Jerusalem heard that Samaria had received the word of God, they sent unto them Peter and John: Who, when they were come down, prayed for them, that they might receive the Holy Ghost: (For as yet he was fallen upon none of them: only they were baptized in the name of the Lord Jesus.) Then laid they their hands upon them and they received the Holy Ghost" (Acts 8:14-17).

Since the Holy Spirit is a gift which is received for the asking and many churches do not teach people that there is an experience called the baptism of the Holy Spirit for which they can ask, many born-again believers repent and are baptized in water without ever receiving the baptism in the Holy Spirit to which they are entitled. "Ye have not, because ye ask not" (James 4:2). Mrs. Meyers, through no fault of her own, was one of these. Probably nobody had ever told her that she *needed* the Holy Spirit. I haven't asked her about it, but I imagine that she may even have thought that as a born-again Christian she had all of the Holy Spirit she was ever going to get. Fortunately, the evangelist she spoke to knew she needed more.

A Spirit-filled Christian is a dynamic Christian. The word translated "power" comes from the Greek word from which we also get the word "dynamite." Thus, one becomes dynamic after he is filled with the Holy Spirit, the Power which God has given him. Keeping filled with the Spirit makes us dynamic in Christian living. When Jesus once stood teaching in the synagogue, he read from the Book of Isaiah the following: "The Spirit of the Lord is upon me, because he hath anointed me to preach the gospel to the poor" (Luke 4:18). We know that we, too, have received this same anointing of the Spirit, for Jesus said in John 14:12, "He that believeth on me, the works that I do shall he do also; and greater works than these shall he do; because I go unto my Father."

What a promise! What a commission! It behooves every one of us to get moving! The Word speaks. We must confess it. We must strengthen our belief by repeating over and over what God has said. Then it becomes our way of life. None of this can happen to the fullest, however, until we open our hearts and become Spirit-filled. Only as the Spirit lives in us can we be effective in our own lives and in the lives of others.

Chapter Eighteen

HIMPOSSIBLE

A young man discovered a vein of gold high up in the mountains. He needed power to develop it. He needed money. He needed to know how to develop the vein. He struggled and worked and failed.

Sitting down one night after a long hard day, tired through and through, he said to himself, "I am finding out what the problem is here, why I simply can't move this thing. I know that gold is *there*, but I can't *get* it. The thing is that I don't know anything about this rock. I don't know anything about geology, and I don't know very much about mining. I am going down to the city and get some answers."

He went down to the city, to the head of the mining department in the university there, and he laid his case honestly and squarely before that expert. That professor called in a mining engineer to whom the young man told his story. The engineer agreed to go with him to see the vein of gold and then to give his advice after seeing the results of tests of the vein.

It took the two men about a week to reach the gold site. After the engineer had explored the mountain and had made certain crude tests of the ore, he said, "There are millions of dollars worth of gold there! But it will cost a great deal of money to get the gold out. You have two choices: you can either organize a stock company to raise enough money to develop the mine, or you can sell this property. Which will you do? The young man answered unhesitatingly, "I am going to develop it."

That young man spent a year in hard training and study. He gave himself completely to it. Through the long winter months, he drove himself until, when the springtime came, he was ready. He had acquired the knowledge that he needed.

The vein proved to be everything that the mining engineer had said that it would be. Within a few short years, that young man had become a millionaire.

This story is a modern parable. That young man discovered that here was something of great value, but he didn't know how to get at it, how to develop it, how to claim its great riches. Then the young man was confronted with making a decision, a choice: take it or leave it. His decision, "I am going to develop it," made the difference. The matter was not closed there, however, for after having spoken the words of his decision, he had to act upon them. It required study, sacrifice, and dedication. At the end of the period of preparation, he reaped the reward for all the days he had spent in getting ready.

Exactly so it is with us in our understanding what place God holds in our lives. You must discover God. This you do by reading and hearing the Word. You go to God—the only One who has the answer for your life. As you study, you will realize the greatness of God's words, but you will also come to realize your own limitations. Then comes the time when you will have to have more than just the knowledge *about* God's promises. You will have to decide, "I am going to develop it." The reward, greater by far than the millions the young man mined, will come as you live out your life in study, dedication, and service.

Matthew 19:26 says, "But Jesus looked at them [His disciples], and said to them, 'With men this is impossible, but *with God all things are possible*'!" There in those words is the answer to any dilemma in which you might ever find yourself. The words that you then choose to believe and to speak will shape your life.

Sometimes when something seems particularly impossible to me, I quote to myself the title of this chapter, "Himpossible." What does it mean? It means, "With men this is impossible, but with God it is possible. I can do all things through Christ Who strengthens me. This is not *im*possible, it's *Him*possible. It's possible with Him."

The trouble with too many people is that they want the fulfillment of God's promises too easily. In Matthew 7:13, Jesus warned, "Enter ye in at the strait gate: for wide is the gate and broad is the way that leadeth to destruction, and many there be which go in thereat: Because strait is the gate, and narrow is the way, which leadeth unto life, and few there be that find it." Jesus Christ is the Gate that leads to life. God expects us to give all of our beings to Him before He can fulfill His promises of great wealth of all kinds. Most of us excuse our inabilities to attain that for which we seek by saying such things as these: "I had a chance, but everything went against me," or "I don't have an education, so I can't expect much," or "I don't know the 'right people.'" Those excuses are the words that God does *not* want to hear. God wants to hear us say, "with God, all things are possible."

One summer we had as our guest, Dr. Len Jones, Director of the Slavic and Oriental Mission of Australia and New Zealand. This man is one of the most stimulating people I have ever met. He is vibrant, optimistic, and consecrated to the Lord. He is tireless in traveling around the world for God.

Standing in the family room of our home, Dr. Jones shared with us an important secret to his success in doing God's work. "Years ago I went to the dictionary and literally crossed out the word 'impossible.' The Bible tells us, 'with God, all things are possible.' Since nothing is impossible with God, and since I have committed my life to Him and am linked with Him, my Father, why should I even regard the word 'impossible?' I consider nothing impossible, for God's Word tells me that. When I repeat those words from God, they become my support in everything that I do."

Matthew 9:27-30 gives an account of Jesus using this principle with two blind men who met Jesus one day as He was leaving Nazareth. These two trusting sightless men followed closely behind Jesus, crying and calling to Him, "Have mercy on us, Son of David."

When Jesus entered the house to which He had been going, the blind men, fearing that He was not going to pay any attention to them, followed. Jesus turned to them and said, "*Do you believe* that I am able to do this?"

"Oh, yes, Lord. We do believe," they cried out together.

Then He touched their eyes and said, "According to your faith, be it done to you."

And their eyes were opened.

Jesus first required their open vocal avowal before He healed those two blind men. He asked them to say in words that they believed. How important were those words! What profit they reaped by fulfilling Jesus' simple request! Jesus knew that they believed, but He wanted to hear them *say* it. Then, knowing that they spoke the truth, He honored them because of their faith.

Some time ago I heard of an experience that a minister had while he was making a tour through a number of foreign countries. The country from which he was taking his departure was almost medieval in its primitive standards of life. All drinking water had to be boiled. All edible fruits had to be peeled. Every traveler had to exercise extreme caution to avoid contracting certain painful diseases that the inhabitants of that country had come to accept as commonplace and unavoidable.

This minister was preparing to *enter* a country that was vastly different. The food there was safe to eat and palatable. The hygienic conditions were irreproachable. The citizens there enjoyed a reasonable degree of prosperity.

"I shall never forget," said the traveler, "how strange it was to step from the rickety bus that brought me to the border so that I could cross the narrow strip of land that separated those two countries. I boarded the modern air-conditioned motor coach on the other side. I accomplished this most welcome transition simply by presenting my passport."

We have passports to God. Our passport is the blood of Jesus Christ. We must use our words to express our honest desire to belong to Him. Then we must show our right to be accepted by declaring our belief in Jesus Christ as our Lord and Savior. We cannot save ourselves by our own efforts, but "with God, all things are possible." If you but realize these truths and affirm them, God will open doors to you that you had formerly thought were impossible barriers. Jesus said, "I am the door; by me if any man enter in, he shall be saved, and shall go in and out, and find pasture (John 10:9). That is the passport He can be in your life: the passport from a life of anxiety in trying to "go it alone" to the life of having all your burdens assumed by Him and all your needs fulfilled.

A woman in Los Angeles told me that she had developed an inner hatred toward her in-laws because of the way they treated her. This is not an uncommon problem. I asked her if she had given God an opportunity to work it out for her. I told her to tell the Lord about it just as frankly and honestly as she had told me. When she did so, she discovered the Spirit of God working in her behalf and helping her.

As she shifted those feelings of resentment from her mind, she experienced a great release. More important, she didn't just half-give those feelings to the Lord and then take them back. When I saw her days later, the whole problem had been given to the Lord; she had left her burden there, and she had discovered that God was taking care of it. As she reached out with greater love to her relatives, she found them reaching back in love to her.

What does God say is His place in *your* life? Psalm 55:22 gives you His words: "Cast thy burden upon the LORD, and he shall sustain thee." That just has to be the greatest weight-lifter the world has ever known. It is matchless! Make those words *your* words, for He says that He will sustain *you*.

You have no need so big or so small that God will not answer if He just hears your request and you fully believe that God will undertake for you. Remember it was *He* who said, "with God, all things are possible."

Austin Barton shared with me this story of a lesson he had learned earlier from an English speaker, Brother Greenwood. He had ministered to Austin Barton with the following directive: "Remember the power of your words. When you ask God for something, don't limit Him. If you need a hundred dollars, say to the Lord, 'I need a hundred dollars *or more*!' If you need two hundred dollars, say to the Lord, 'I need two hundred dollars *or more*.' If you need a thousand dollars, say to the

Lord, 'I need a thousand dollars *or more*.' But give the Lord the opportunity to do abundantly that which you ask."

I agree that our words will produce exactly what we say. If you're living a paltry life, resolve today to change it. After resolving to change it, talk about it to God, talk about it everywhere! Expect great things to happen, for God will be your Provider. He will be—if *your words* will it. What you say determines what you get.

Often we become our own problem. Instead of being part of the answer, we continue to be part of the problem. Suppose your senses have revealed that you are in great need financially. The Word declares, "My God shall supply all your need" (Philippians 4:19). You need to call God's attention to the missing finances. You need to be sure that your expectations are from Him. Refuse to be intimidated by your feelings. Know that greater is God who is in you than all the other forces that surround you. The forces that oppose you are your senses, your feelings. The power that is *in* you is God working in your life.

Then speak out. Make your words express the truth about what God means to you, about your union and partnership with God. Affirm that He is the One who backs you up and furnishes the capital to fulfill your needs. Give Him credit for His ability and His wisdom. Dare to confess aloud for the world to hear that your confidence for success lies in His grace as He has shown it to you. God will honor such commitment. Only with Him do all things become possible.

I recall a woman who was attending one of our

meetings. Many people had prayed for her, but she continued to bear her own burden. One day I preached on the subject that Satan seeks to keep you sin-conscious. This hinders your faith, and of course that is exactly what Satan is attempting to do every day of your life. He does this by raising doubt in your mind. He will tell you that God has never forgiven you for what you have done. Or he tells you that there is too much sin in your life to please God.

This woman, who identified herself as Mrs. Blaine, approached me after service. She was obviously a troubled person. She poured out to me her many attempts to be healed. Then she blurted out, "But now I know why my faith won't produce results. I committed a terrible sin twenty-five years ago, and God has never forgiven me."

I questioned her, "Can you tell me what that sin was?"

She responded, "I lied about one of my relatives. I suggested to her husband that she was not being faithful to him. The terrible trouble that followed almost caused those two to separate, and there were rifts in my whole family because of my remarks."

I gave her the words of 1 John 1:9: "If we confess our sins"—*That* is *our* part in this divine transaction: to confess our sins to God.—"God is faithful and just to forgive us our sins and to cleanse us from all unrighteousness." *That* is *God's* part!

Mrs. Blaine, continuing, replied, "But, Brother Gossett, I've cried, and I've prayed many times to God to forgive me that terrible wrong I committed, but He never has."

My response was quick and sharp. "Mrs. Blaine, I

don't believe that you realize what you are saying! When you tell me that you have confessed your sin to God, and that He hasn't forgiven you, you are contradicting God. What you are saying is not true. Let God be true, and every man a liar. God is not a *man*, that He should lie. God will do what He *says*. God keeps His Word."

Then she appealed to me, "What must I do then?"

"Simply take God at His Word," I stated. "Since God has said that He would be faithful and just to forgive and cleanse all sins when we confess them to Him, take Him at His Word. Whether you *feel* forgiveness or not, God has promised it, and it is so. Begin to thank Him for His grace and mercy."

That woman went off alone to pray. Later, when I saw her again, she was praising God for the assurance that her sins—even dating back twenty-five years—were all forgiven!

When you state a thing, you actually decree that thing into your life. If you decree that you have no forgiveness, you will have no forgiveness. But if you decree that God's supply is yours, then you will *have* His supply. In Mark 11, Jesus said, "Whoever shall say . . . and not doubt in his heart, but shall believe that those things which he saith shall come to pass; he shall have whatsoever he saith."

By your *words*, you establish in your life the exact place that God will hold. Your prayer should be, "Let the words of my mouth and the meditations of my heart be acceptable in thy sight, O LORD, my strength and my redeemer" (Psalm 19:14). Meditate much, but see that your meditations are governed by the Word of God. Your conduct is largely made up of past thinking. You cannot think or meditate long and deeply without your thoughts materializing into action and words.

How very important it is that you yield to God the very first place in your life! You will be yielding your mind and spirit as channels through which God can think *His* thoughts. For that we do thank and praise the Lord!

DON'T PUT IT OFF
AND DON'T GIVE UP

1. Always expect the best—always. Don't expect the worst—ever. Expect a miracle. It is your attitude toward life that makes your life. You always get exactly what you expect...good or evil. Expect the good and you will get it—expect the bad, and you will get that also.

2. By your prayerful expectancy right now you are deciding what you and your circumstances will be tomorrow. The man at the Beautiful Gate "gave heed unto them, expecting to receive something of them." He expected something and got it. Expect miracles for your life, and miracles will be your portion, even as a miracle was the portion for the hopeless cripple at the gate.

3. Be one who says, "God can do things and God will do things...through me." This is not egotism; it is one hundred percent scriptural. Hebrews 11 tells us of men and women who did things. You too can do things—whatever the Lord wants done.

4. The secret of victory is action and persistence. Don't put it off and don't give up. "The violent shall take it by force" (Matthew 11:12). This violent faith always takes things!

5. You live NOW, today, never in "tomorrow." Don't say what you would do if circumstances were in your favor, or if you had the money, or if you had the education, or if you had the opportunities. Wipe out that "if" and go on and conquer. Cease dreaming about the good life you may have next year, or ten years from now. Begin to live at your best right now.

6. Be great for God *now*. Forgive others *now*. Be bold and fearless *now*. Don't postpone positive and constructive living to some vague and indefinite future.

7. Refuse to be dominated by fear. "The thing which I greatly feared is come upon me, and that which I was afraid of is come unto me" (Job 3:25). Whatever you continually fear, you will get. Don't blame it on bad luck, misfortune, fate or "other people." You ask for it yourself, by giving place to fear. You are your own biggest enemy, your biggest troublemaker. Sure enough, the thing you fear will come upon you. Change all this right now: affirm it. "Fear has no part in my heart, for God has not given me the spirit of fear!"

PART II

WHAT YOU GET

HOW TO USE THESE PROMISES

We have devoted most of this book to *What You Say*, and I trust that you have read and used many Bible promises already. The rest of this book is dessert: it is entirely devoted to Scripture promises you can claim using the principles of speaking and believing which we have already discussed.

As a review, I want to remind you that when you took Jesus as your Lord, you became a child of God. Like all of God's children, you now have certain rights and privileges, which are spelled out for you in God's Word, the Bible.

Although the covenant you have with God is the New Covenant, you may also claim any promise granted under the Old Covenant, since the Bible tells us that "*all* the promises of God in him [Christ] are yea, and in him Amen, unto the glory of God by us." If it's in the Bible, it's a promise you can claim!

God says, "My covenant will I not break, nor alter the thing that is gone out of my lips" (Psalm 89:34); "I have spoken it, I will also bring it to pass; I have purposed it, I will also do it" (Isaiah 46:11). The Bible tells us that God cannot lie, and that what He has promised, He is also able to perform. Therefore, when you claim a promise from the Bible (fulfilling any conditions attached to it), you can know without a shadow of a doubt that God will keep His Word in the matter.

It is important to take each promise exactly as it reads. Don't try to add to it, or explain what "it must really mean," or read between the lines. Read it just exactly as though it were a legal document—because that's what it is. The Bible is the testament (or will) which explains all that we inherited when Christ died for us.

If there is a part of a promise that mentions something you must do ("pray," "believe," etc.), then do it. There are some promises God regards as a bargain—they tell what He will do once you fulfill your part of the deal.

Finally, remember that God has promised *what* He will do, but He hasn't promised *when* He will do it—although He always does "it" in time! The desired results may come immediately. Then again—they may not. The Bible calls this waiting period "the trying of our faith," and says that it "worketh patience" (James 1:3), and that it is "much more precious than of gold that perisheth" (1 Peter 1:7). But fear not, only believe, and God will cause the desired result to come to pass in His perfect timing.

Here, now, is *What You Get*.

ANSWERS TO PRAYER

With God, nothing is impossible. Here are promises from the Word of God that you can claim whenever you need a miracle answer to prayer.

For every one that asketh receiveth; and he that seeketh findeth; and to him that knocketh it shall be opened (Matthew 7:8).

If ye then, being evil, know how to give good gifts unto your children, how much more shall your Father which is in heaven give good things to them that ask him? (Matthew 7:11).

If ye have faith as a grain of mustard seed, ye shall say unto this mountain, Remove hence to yonder place; and it shall remove; and nothing shall be impossible unto you (Matthew 17:20).

Again I say unto you, That if two of you shall agree on earth as touching any thing that they shall ask, it shall be done for them of my Father which is in heaven (Matthew 18:19).

And all things, whatsoever ye shall ask in prayer, believing, ye shall receive (Matthew 21:22).

If thou canst believe, all things are possible to him that believeth (Mark 9:23).

And Jesus answering saith unto them, Have faith in God. For verily I say unto you, That whosoever shall say unto this mountain, Be thou removed, and be thou cast into the sea; and shall not doubt in his heart, but shall believe that those things which he saith shall come to pass; he shall have whatsoever he saith. Therefore I say unto you, What things soever ye desire, when ye pray, believe that ye receive them, and ye shall have them (Mark 11:22-24).

And these signs shall follow them that believe; In my name shall they cast out devils; they shall speak with new tongues; They shall take up serpents; and if they drink any deadly thing, it shall not hurt them; they shall lay hands on the sick, and they shall recover (Mark 16:17-18).

And the Lord said, If ye had faith as a grain of mustard seed, ye might say unto this sycamine tree, Be thou plucked up by the root, and be thou planted in the sea; and it should obey you (Luke 17:6).

He that believeth on me, the words that I do shall he do also; and greater works than these shall he do; because I go unto my Father (John 14:12).

And whatsoever ye shall ask in my name, that will I do, that the Father may be glorified in the Son (John 14:13).

If ye shall ask any thing in my name, I will do it (John 14:14).

Whatsoever ye shall ask of the Father in my name, he may give it you (John 15:16).

At that day ye shall ask in my name: and I say not unto you, that I will pray the Father for you: For the Father himself loveth you, because ye have loved me, and have believed that I came out from God (John 16:26-27).

THE BAPTISM OF
THE HOLY SPIRIT

The baptism of the Holy Spirit is the greatest secret to a life that gets what it says. It is a second experience with God (the first is being born-again) in which the Christian begins to receive a new infilling of supernatural power in his life. Here are scriptures which show that you can expect to be filled with the Holy Spirit:

I will put my spirit within you, and cause you to walk in my statutes, and ye shall keep my judgments, and do them (Ezekiel 36:27).

It shall come to pass afterward, that I will pour out my spirit upon all flesh; and your sons and your daughters shall prophesy, your old men shall dream dreams, your young men shall see visions (Joel 2:28).

I indeed baptize you with water unto repentance: but he that cometh after me is mightier than I, whose shoes I am not worthy to bear: he shall baptize you with the Holy Ghost, and with fire (Matthew 3:11).

If ye then, being evil, know how to give good gifts unto your children: how much more shall your heavenly Father give the Holy Spirit to them that ask him? (Luke 11:13).

I will pray the Father, and he shall give you another Comforter, that he may abide with you for ever; Even the Spirit of truth; whom the world cannot receive, because it seeth him not, neither knoweth him: but ye know him; for he dwelleth with you, and shall be in you (John 14:16, 17).

But the Comforter, which is the Holy Ghost, whom the Father will send in my name, he shall teach you all things, and bring all things to your remembrance, whatsoever I have said unto you (John 14:26).

But when the Comforter is come, whom I will send unto you from the Father, even the Spirit of truth, which proceedeth from the Father, he shall testify of me (John 15:26).

Nevertheless I tell you the truth; It is expedient for you that I go away: for if I go not away, the Comforter will not come unto you; but if I depart, I will send him unto you (John 16:7).

Ye shall receive power, after that the Holy Ghost is come upon you: and ye shall be witnesses unto me both in Jerusalem, and in all Judaea, and in Samaria, and unto the uttermost part of the earth (Acts 1:8).

Repent, and be baptized every one of you in the name of Jesus Christ for the remission of sins, and ye shall receive the gift of the Holy Ghost (Acts 2:38).

For the promise is unto you, and to your children, and to all that are afar off, even as many as the Lord our God shall call (Acts 2:39).

COMFORT

Jesus wants us to have peace and joy even in the midst of adversity and testing. Here are fourteen reasons why you should not grieve, but rather have confidence and rejoice for the Lord's wonderful provisions for you:

Thou shalt forget thy misery, and remember it as waters that pass away (Job 11:16).

Yea, though I walk through the valley of the shadow of death, I will fear no evil: for thou art with me; thy rod and thy staff they comfort me (Psalm 23:4).

The LORD is nigh unto them that are of a broken heart; and saveth such as be of a contrite spirit (Psalm 34:18).

This is my comfort in my affliction: for thy word hath quickened me (Psalm 119:50).

He healeth the broken in heart, and bindeth up their wounds (Psalm 147:3).

The LORD hath comforted his people, and will have mercy upon his afflicted (Isaiah 49:13).

I, even I, am he that comforteth you (Isaiah 51:12).

For the mountains shall depart, and the hills be removed; but my kindness shall not depart from thee, neither shall the covenant of my peace be removed, saith the LORD that hath mercy on thee (Isaiah 54:10).

He hath sent me to bind up the brokenhearted ... to comfort all that mourn; to appoint unto them that mourn in Zion, to give them beauty for ashes, the oil of joy for mourning, the garment of praise for the spirit of heaviness (Isaiah 61:1, 2, 3).

Blessed are they that mourn: for they shall be comforted (Matthew 5:4).

I will not leave you comfortless: I will come to you (John 14:18).

Blessed be God, even the Father of our Lord Jesus Christ, the Father of mercies, and the God of all comfort; who comforteth us in all our tribulation, that we may be able to comfort them which are in any trouble, by the comfort wherewith we ourselves are comforted of God (2 Corinthians 1:3, 4).

FAITH

You can be bold in your Christian life through knowing that you are a faith man, a faith woman. You can claim the faith you need for any situation. What a blessing to know for sure that—no matter how you may feel—God says that faith is something you already have. It is a gift from Him!

For therein is the righteousness of God revealed from faith to faith: as it is written, The just shall live by faith (Romans 1:17).

Faith cometh by hearing, and hearing by the word of God (Romans 10:17).

God hath dealt to every man the measure of faith (Romans 12:3).

But the scripture hath concluded all under sin, that the promise by faith of Jesus Christ might be given to them that believe (Galatians 3:22).

For ye are all the children of God by faith in Christ Jesus (Galatians 3:26).

The fruit of the Spirit is love, joy, peace, longsuffering, gentleness, goodness, faith, meekness, temperance (Galatians 5:22, 23).

For by grace are ye saved through faith; and that not of yourselves: it is the gift of God (Ephesians 2:8).

Unto you it is given in the behalf of Christ...to believe on him (Philippians 1:29).

Be not slothful, but followers of them who through faith and patience inherit the promises (Hebrews 6:12).

Whatsoever is born of God overcometh the world: and this is the victory that overcometh the world, even our faith (1 John 5:4).

FELLOWSHIP WITH GOD

The Bible tells us that God created us for His pleasure—that "such as are upright in their way are his delight" (Proverbs 11:20). If we obey Him, we may be God's friends.

The LORD is with you, while ye be with him; and if ye seek him, he will be found of you (2 Chronicles 15:2).

The upright shall dwell in thy presence (Psalm 140:13).

And, lo I am with you always, even unto the end of the world (Matthew 28:20).

He that hath my commandments and keepeth them, he it is that loveth me: and he that loveth me shall be loved of my Father, and I will love him, and will manifest myself to him (John 14:21).

Ye are my friends, if ye do whatsoever I command you (John 15:14).

Draw nigh to God, and he will draw nigh to you (James 4:8).

That which we have seen and heard declare we unto you, that ye also may have fellowship with us: and truly our fellowship is with the Father, and with his Son Jesus Christ (1 John 1:3).

Behold, I stand at the door, and knock: if any man hear my voice, and open the door, I will come in to him, and will sup with him, and he with me (Revelation 3:20).

FINANCIAL PROSPERITY

Freedom from financial worries is assured by God's Word. Many people are robbed of peace and joy in the Lord because of their constant worry about finances. As a Christian, however, if you are faithful in your tithes and offerings, you can claim the promises below. Banks may close and money may be devaluated, but God's Word is sure forever.

Keep therefore the words of this covenant, and do them, that ye may prosper in all that ye do (Deuteronomy 29:9).

Trust in the LORD, and do good; so shalt thou dwell in the land, and verily thou shalt be fed (Psalm 37:3).

I have been young, and now am old; yet have I not seen the righteous forsaken, nor His seed begging bread (Psalm 37:25).

The LORD will give grace and glory: no good thing will he withhold from them that walk uprightly (Psalm 84:11).

A good man leaveth an inheritance to his children's children: and the wealth of the sinner is laid up for the just (Proverbs 13:22).

Cast thy bread upon the waters: for thou shalt find it after many days (Ecclesiastes 11:1).

I will give thee the treasures of darkness, and hidden

riches of secret places, that thou mayest know that I, the LORD, which call thee by name, am the God of Israel (Isaiah 45:3).

Give, and it shall be given unto you; good measure, pressed down, and shaken together, and running over, shall men give into your bosom. For with the same measure that ye mete withal it shall be measured to you again (Luke 6:38).

If then God so clothe the grass, which is today in the field, and tomorrow is cast into the oven; how much more will he clothe you? (Luke 12:28).

But rather seek ye the kingdom of God; and all these things shall be added unto you (Luke 12:31).

Fear not, little flock; for it is your Father's good pleasure to give you the kingdom (Luke 12:32).

Hitherto have ye asked nothing in my name: ask, and ye shall receive, that your joy may be full (John 16:24).

But my God shall supply all your need according to his riches in glory by Christ Jesus (Philippians 4:19).

Beloved, I wish above all things that thou mayest prosper and be in health, even as thy soul prospereth (3 John 2).

FORGIVENESS

If you will forgive those who have wronged you, God will forgive you when you need forgiveness. First forgive; then ask forgiveness; then stand on the following promises.

As far as the east is from the west, so far hath he removed our transgressions from us (Psalm 103:12).

There is therefore now no condemnation to them which are in Christ Jesus, who walk not after the flesh, but after the Spirit (Romans 8:1).

And such were some of you: but ye are washed, but ye are sanctified, but ye are justified in the name of the Lord Jesus, and by the Spirit of our God (1 Corinthians 6:11).

For he hath made him to be sin for us, who knew no sin; that we might be made the righteousness of God in him (2 Corinthians 5:21).

In whom we have redemption through his blood, the forgiveness of sins, according to the riches of his grace (Ephesians 1:7).

In whom we have redemption through his blood, even the forgiveness of sins (Colossians 1:14).

But if we walk in the light, as he is in the light, we have fellowship one with another, and the blood of Jesus Christ his Son cleanseth us from all sin (1 John 1:7).

If we confess our sins, he is faithful and just to forgive us our sins, and to cleanse us from all unrighteousness (1 John 1:9).

If any man sin, we have an advocate with the Father, Jesus Christ the righteous: And he is the propitiation for our sins: and not for ours only, but also for the sins of the whole world (1 John 2:1, 2).

HEALING

"Fear not, only believe." I have seen God heal thousands of people, and what He did for them He'll do for you.

I am the LORD that healeth thee (Exodus 15:26).

I will take sickness away from the midst of thee (Exodus 23:25).

Bless the LORD, O my soul, and forget not all his benefits: Who forgiveth all thine iniquities; who healeth all thy diseases; who redeemeth thy life from destruction (Psalm 103:2-4).

He sent his word and healed them (Psalm 107:20).

With his stripes we are healed (Isaiah 53:5).

Unto you that fear my name shall the Sun of righteousness arise with healing in his wings (Malachi 4:2).

Himself took our infirmities and bare our sicknesses (Matthew 8:17).

These signs shall follow them that believe ... they shall lay hands on the sick, and they shall recover (Mark 16:17, 18).

Is any sick among you? let him call for the elders of the church; and let them pray over him, anointing him with oil in the name of the Lord: And the prayer of faith shall save the sick, and the Lord shall raise him up; and if he have committed sins, they shall be forgiven him (James 5:14, 15).

Confess your faults one to another, and pray one for another, that ye may be healed (James 5:16).

By whose stripes ye were healed (1 Peter 2:24).

Beloved, I wish above all things that thou mayest prosper and be in health, even as thy soul prospereth (3 John 2).

HEAVENLY REWARDS

Since God's Word says that He will give heavenly rewards to Christians, you might as well put in a reservation for yours right now. Claim that God will cause you to live in such a way that you will be eligible for the very best ones!

As for me, I will behold thy face in righteousness: I shall be satisfied, when I awake, with thy likeness (Psalm 17:15).

But lay up for yourselves treasures in heaven, where neither moth nor rust doth corrupt, and where thieves do not break through nor steal (Matthew 6:20).

Then shall the righteous shine forth as the sun in the kingdom of their father (Matthew 13:43).

His Lord said unto him, Well done, thou good and faithful servant: thou hast been faithful over a few things, I will make thee ruler over many things: enter thou into the joy of thy lord (Matthew 25:21).

Then shall the King say unto them on his right hand, Come, ye blessed of my Father, inherit the kingdom prepared for you from the foundation of the world (Matthew 25:34).

In my Father's house are many mansions: if it were not so, I would have told you. I go to prepare a place for you. And if I go and prepare a place for you, I will come again, and receive you unto myself; that where I am, there ye may be also (John 14:2, 3).

When Christ, who is our life, shall appear, then shall ye also appear with him in glory (Colossians 3:4).

So shall we ever be with the Lord (1 Thessalonians 4:17).

There is laid up for me a crown of righteousness, which the Lord, the righteous judge, shall give me at that day: and not to me only, but unto all them also that love his appearing (2 Timothy 4:8).

They desire a better country, that is, an heavenly: wherefore God is not ashamed to be called their God: for he hath prepared for them a city (Hebrews 11:16).

We, according to his promise, look for new heavens and a new earth, wherein dwelleth righteousness (2 Peter 3:13).

They are before the throne of God, and serve him day and night in his temple: and he that sitteth on the throne shall dwell among them. They shall hunger no more, neither thirst any more; neither shall the sun light on them, nor any heat. For the Lamb which is in the midst of the throne shall feed them, and shall lead them unto living fountains of waters: and God shall wipe away all tears from their eyes (Revelation 7:15-17).

There shall be no night there; and they need no candle, neither light of the sun; for the Lord God giveth them light: and they shall reign for ever and ever (Revelation 22:5).

HELP

There are some people whose help I don't need! But God's help is the best there is. Here are scriptures which promise His help to you.

Our soul waiteth for the LORD: he is our help and our shield (Psalm 33:20).

God is our refuge and strength, a very present help in trouble (Psalm 46:1).

Ye that fear the LORD, trust in the LORD: he is their help and their shield (Psalm 115:11).

My help cometh from the LORD, which made heaven and earth (Psalm 121:2).

Our help is in the name of the LORD, who made heaven and earth (Psalm 124:8).

Fear thou not; for I am with thee: be not dismayed; for I am thy God: I will strengthen thee; yea, I will help thee; yea, I will uphold thee with the right hand of my righteousness (Isaiah 41:10).

Likewise the Spirit also helpeth our infirmities: for we know not what we should pray for as we ought: but the Spirit itself maketh intercession for us with groanings which cannot be uttered (Romans 8:26).

Let us therefore come boldly unto the throne of grace, that we may obtain mercy, and find grace to help in time of need (Hebrews 4:16).

So that we may boldly say, The Lord is my helper, and I will not fear what man shall do unto me (Hebrews 13:6).

POWER

The power that God gives is power to serve. For "Whosoever of you will be the chiefest, shall be the servant of all."

The God of Israel is he that giveth strength and power unto his people (Psalm 68:35).

He giveth power to the faint; and to them that have no might he increaseth strength (Isaiah 40:29).

Behold, I give unto you power to tread on serpents and scorpions, and over all the power of the enemy: and nothing shall by any means hurt you (Luke 10:19).

Verily, verily, I say unto you, He that believeth on me, the works that I do shall he do also; and greater works than these shall he do; because I go unto my Father (John 14:12).

Ye shall receive power, after that the Holy Ghost is come upon you (Acts 1:8).

If God be for us, who can be against us? (Romans 8:31).

For God hath not given us the spirit of fear; but of power, and of love, and of a sound mind (2 Timothy 1:7).

PROTECTION

The Bible tells us that God is able to protect His children both from sudden calamity and from known hazards.

Thou art my hiding place; thou shalt preserve me from trouble; thou shalt compass me about with songs of deliverance (Psalm 32:7).

The angel of the LORD encampeth round about them that fear him, and delivereth them (Psalm 34:7).

There shall no evil befall thee, neither shall any plague come nigh thy dwelling (Psalm 91:10).

The LORD shall preserve thee from all evil: he shall preserve thy soul (Psalm 121:7).

Though I walk in the midst of trouble, thou wilt revive me: thou shalt stretch forth thine hand against the wrath of mine enemies, and thy right hand shall save me (Psalm 138:7).

For the LORD shall be thy confidence, and shall keep thy foot from being taken (Proverbs 3:26).

If God be for us, who can be against us? (Romans 8:31).

But the Lord is faithful, who shall stablish you, and keep you from evil (2 Thessalonians 3:3).

SALVATION

God wants to save you just as much as you want to be saved, and He has promised that "If any man hear my voice and open the door, I will come in to him."

And she shall bring forth a son, and thou shalt call his name JESUS: for he shall save his people from their sins (Matthew 1:21).

For God so loved the world, that he gave his only begotten Son, that whosoever believeth in him should not perish, but have everlasting life (John 3:16).

All that the Father giveth me shall come to me; and him that cometh to me I shall in no wise cast out (John 6:37).

I am the door: by me if any man enter in, he shall be saved, and shall go in and out, and find pasture (John 10:9).

Jesus said unto her, I am the resurrection, and the life: he that believeth in me, though he were dead, yet shall he live (John 11:25).

Jesus saith unto him, I am the way, the truth, and the life: no man cometh unto the Father, but by me (John 14:6).

And this is life eternal, that they might know thee the only true God, and Jesus Christ, whom thou hast sent (John 17:3).

The wages of sin is death; but the gift of God is eternal life through Jesus Christ our Lord (Romans 6:23).

For whosoever shall call upon the name of the Lord shall be saved (Romans 10:13).

SPIRITUAL WELFARE

The Bible says that we are all being transformed to be like Jesus, "from glory to glory." God has promised both to keep us and to cause us to grow in Him.

The LORD will perfect that which concerneth me (Psalm 138:8).

The path of the just is as the shining light, that shineth more and more unto the perfect day (Proverbs 4:18).

And this is the Father's will which hath sent me, that of all which he hath given me I should lose nothing, but should raise it up again at the last day (John 6:39).

My sheep hear my voice, and I know them, and they follow me: And I give unto them eternal life; and they shall never perish, neither shall any man pluck them out of my hand (John 10:27-28).

Who shall also confirm you unto the end, that ye may be blameless in the day of our Lord Jesus Christ (1 Corinthians 1:8).

But we all, with open face beholding as in a glass the glory of the Lord, are changed into the same image from glory to glory, even as by the Spirit of the Lord (2 Corinthians 3:18).

He which hath begun a good work in you will perform it until the day of Jesus Christ (Philippians 1:6).

Who are kept by the power of God through faith unto salvation ready to be revealed in the last time (1 Peter 1:5).

STRENGTH

God has promised us strength for our bodies and strength for our spirits; in addition, He is ever present to lend us His strength, the greatest strength of all!

The joy of the Lord is your strength (Nehemiah 8:10).

He that hath clean hands shall be stronger and stronger (Job 17:9).

The LORD will give strength unto his people (Psalm 29:11).

But the salvation of the righteous is of the LORD: he is their strength in time of trouble (Psalm 37:39).

The God of Israel is he that giveth strength and power unto his people (Psalm 68:35).

Trust ye in the LORD for ever: for in the LORD JEHOVAH is everlasting strength (Isaiah 26:4).

But they that wait upon the LORD shall renew their strength; they shall mount up with wings as eagles; they shall run, and not be weary; and they shall walk, and not faint (Isaiah 40:31).

The people that do know their God shall be strong and do exploits (Daniel 11:32).

Let the weak say, I am strong (Joel 3:10).

I can do all things through Christ which strengtheneth me (Philippians 4:13).

WISDOM

The most important wisdom God gives is wisdom to know His will. But his promises are unqualified. A loving Father, He yearns to help us with wisdom for even our smallest problems.

For the LORD giveth wisdom: out of his mouth cometh knowledge and understanding. He layeth up sound wisdom for the righteous (Proverbs 2:6, 7).

They that seek the LORD understand all things (Proverbs 28:5).

For God giveth to a man that is good in his sight, wisdom, and knowledge, and joy (Ecclesiastes 2:26).

Call unto me, and I will answer thee, and show thee great and mighty things, which thou knowest not (Jeremiah 33:3).

If a man will do his will, he shall know of the doctrine (John 7:17).

And ye shall know the truth (John 8:32).

But the Comforter, which is the Holy Ghost, whom the Father will send in my name, he shall teach you all things, and bring all things to your remembrance, whatsoever I have said unto you (John 14:26).

Howbeit when he, the Spirit of truth, is come, he will guide you into all truth . . . he will shew you things to come (John 16:13).

But of him are ye in Christ Jesus, who of God is made unto us wisdom, and righteousness, and sanctification, and redemption (1 Corinthians 1:30).

But we have the mind of Christ (1 Corinthians 2:16).

For this is good and acceptable in the sight of God our Saviour; Who will have all men to be saved, and to come unto the knowledge of the truth (1 Timothy 2:3, 4).

If any of you lack wisdom, let him ask of God, that giveth to all men liberally, and upbraideth not; and it shall be given unto him (James 1:5).